SPIDERS

OF SOUTHERN AFRICA

Astri & John Leroy

Struik Nature
(an imprint of Random House Struik (Pty) Ltd)
Reg. No. 1966/003153/07
80 McKenzie Street, Cape Town, 8001
PO Box 1144, Cape Town, 8000 South Africa

Visit us at
www.randomstruik.co.za
Log on to our photographic website
www.imagesofafrica.co.za
for an African experience

First published as *Spiderwatch in Southern Africa* in 2000.
Second Edition titled *Spiders of Southern Africa* published in 2003.

5 7 9 10 8 6

Publishing manager: Pippa Parker
Managing editor: Simon Pooley
Editor: Helena Reid
Designer: Dominic Robson
Cover design: David du Plessis
Illustrators: Steven Felmore (pp. 8, 19, 22, 42–43, 60, 89),
and the Authors
Proofreader: Brenda Brickman
Consultant: Dr Ansie Dippenaar-Schoeman

Reproduction by Hirt and Carter, Cape (Pty) Ltd
Printed and bound by Kyodo Nation Printing Services Co.,Ltd

ISBN 978 1 86872 944 9

Front cover: *Namaqua baboon spider,* Harpactira namaquensis.
Back cover: *Ogre-faced spider,* Deinopsis *sp.*
Half-title: *Yellow lynx spider (family Oxyopidae), and prey.*

CONTENTS

AUTHORS' ACKNOWLEDGEMENTS

The contents of this book have been drawn from many sources: personal observations, field experience, interaction with arachnologists, books and scientific publications. Many people have also contributed, and if we leave anyone out, please forgive us. Ansie Dippenaar-Schoeman, who gave a lot of technical advice and read through, commented on and corrected the manuscript, merits special attention. Werner Croucamp read through and commented on the section on 'Dangerous Spiders'. Paul Seldon supplied background information for the chapter on 'Spider Evolution' and read through and commented on the finished chapter. Thanks too must go to Norman Larsen, who put the publishers in touch with us in the first place. Members of the Spider Club of Southern Africa – too many to thank individually – have contributed generously, even if they were not always aware of it. To them all, spider people past and present, thank you for friendships forged and for what we have learnt together and taught one another about spiders – it has been invaluable.

This book would not have been possible without the support and encouragement we received from each other, and the time and space we allowed each other to work on this project. We spent weeks together reading through, discussing and commenting on the draft manuscript. Astri did most of the writing, while John took all but one of the photographs, helped with the drawings and wrote the section on photography.

Finally, thanks must go to Pippa Parker and Helena Reid of Struik New Holland Publishers for their patience and support – without them we would have given up long ago.

Astri and John Leroy

Opposite: *The orb web of a silver marsh spider,* Leucauge *sp. (family Tetragnathidae), has an open hub and is usually constructed in vegetation.*

INTRODUCTION

Many people think that spiders have too many legs; that they're probably deadly poisonous, dirty, and that they build ugly webs in neglected corners. This is entirely untrue. Spiders are, in fact, clean creatures with varied and intriguing lifestyles.

Some spiders are beautiful, others cheekily enchanting, and many build webs that are exquisitely intricate. They're useful too, and help to keep insect numbers in check. In essence, spiders are small, predatory animals with eight jointed legs, external skeletons, two main body parts and simple eyes. They produce silk, lay eggs and do not metamorphose. Unless you live in polar regions, there is at least one, probably more, not very far from you right now. However, they have no intention whatsoever to harm you.

The questions most commonly asked about spiders are: How poisonous are they? How many are deadly? And what's the biggest spider in the world? But if you want to appreciate spiders you should rather learn to ask:

What spider is that? What do spiders eat? And how do they build their webs? This book has been designed to answer these and other questions, to allay fears and debunk myths, and, in the process, will hopefully generate a greater awareness of these fascinating creatures.

SOUTHERN AFRICA

The southern African subregion comprises South Africa, Lesotho, Swaziland, Namibia, Botswana, Zimbabwe and Mozambique south of the Zambezi River. Although in this book the main emphasis is on spiders from the southern African subregion, interesting facts about spiders from the rest of Africa and other continents have also been included.

Southern Africa encompasses an enormous variety of habitats, which is one of the reasons why so many different spiders are found here compared to most other regions of the world. The southern African region ranges from tropical lowlands to windswept mountain peaks, from wetlands to deserts, forests, grasslands, bushveld, seashores and woodlands. Some habitats have been severely altered by humans, while other true wilderness areas remain unspoilt. The climate ranges from arid to humid, includes summer- and winter-rainfall areas, and creates local variations such as snowfalls in the high mountains and extreme heat in the desert areas. Spiders live in all these places and under all these conditions.

Humans have been fascinated by spiders since prehistoric times, as illustrated by this painting in Battle Cave in the Drakensberg, KwaZulu-Natal. Top: Horned baboon spider, Ceratogyrus brachycephalus *(family Theraphosidae).*

At present, the southern African region supports 64 of the 106 spider families known to occur worldwide. They represent approximately 3 800 recorded species, which range in size from a gigantic (for spiders) 60 mm to a tiny 0,48 mm, and include spiders that live along the shoreline, 'swim' in desert sand, 'cartwheel' down dunes to escape predators, and mimic ants and wasps to fool their enemies. Some of the region's male spiders tie their partners down before mating, while others stroke their mates' abdomens to get them 'in the mood'; one family (Uloboridae) has no venom glands at all, while some species of black button spiders are among the most venomous spiders in the world. The majority of spiders found in the region, however, are small, inoffensive creatures that keep mostly to themselves.

WHERE SPIDERS FIT IN

In many people's minds all land invertebrates (animals without backbones) are grouped together as 'bugs' or '*goggas*', and are lumped together under the name 'insects'. Although insects are the largest group of land invertebrates, they are definitely not the only one. Invertebrates with an outer skeleton, or exoskeleton, and jointed appendages are known as arthropods. There are many arthropod orders, some of the main ones illustrated in the arthropod 'tree' on page 8. As shown, insects and arachnids are only very distantly related, and are on different 'branches' of the tree. The branch that insects are found on represents the mandibulata, arthropods with antennae, while spiders are found on the chelicerata branch, which represents arthropods without antennae or wings.

Arachnids are animals with four pairs of legs, no wings, two body parts (except for mites, which have one main body part) and pincer- or claw-like jaws. Spiders belong to this class, but are separated from their fellow arachnids by having the two main body parts joined by a stalk, or pedicel, and by the fact that they usually have eight simple eyes and an abdomen that has little or no segmentation.

BIGGEST AND SMALLEST

Certain tropical spiders grow very large. A South American tarantula or bird-eating spider, *Theraphosa blondi*, found in Venezuela, Brazil and Guyana may hold the record – a captive specimen has reputedly reached a body length of 100 mm. With readily available food and safety from predators, they probably grow bigger in captivity because they simply carry on growing until they die of old age.

Citharischius crawshayi from East Africa – a hefty spider reaching a body length of about 75 mm – held the African record for many years. This record, however, has been broken by *Hysterocrates hercules,* from Upper Niger in West Africa, with a recorded body length of 90 mm. Our own baboon spiders are outclassed by these 'monsters', the biggest recorded being 60 mm.

The world's smallest spider also hails from the African continent. The adult female dwarf orb weaver, *Anapistula caecula* (family Symphytognathidae), from the Ivory Coast, measures a mere 0,48 mm and is too small to illustrate here.

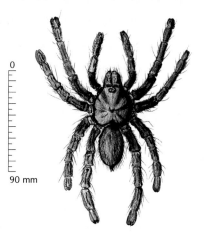

0

90 mm

Hysterocrates hercules (Theraphosidae), *the African continent's largest spider.*

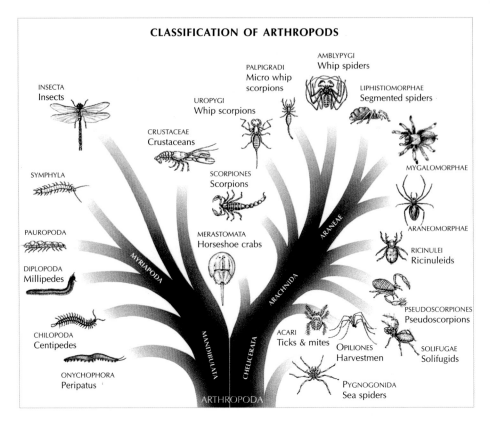

CLASSIFICATION OF ARTHROPODS

AMBLYPYGI
Whip spiders

PALPIGRADI
Micro whip scorpions

LIPHISTIOMORPHAE
Segmented spiders

INSECTA
Insects

UROPYGI
Whip scorpions

CRUSTACEAE
Crustaceans

MYGALOMORPHAE

SYMPHYLA

SCORPIONES
Scorpions

ARANEOMORPHAE

PAUROPODA

MERASTOMATA
Horseshoe crabs

RICINULEI
Ricinuleids

DIPLOPODA
Millipedes

PSEUDOSCORPIONES
Pseudoscorpions

CHILOPODA
Centipedes

ACARI
Ticks & mites

OPILIONES
Harvestmen

SOLIFUGAE
Solifugids

ONYCHOPHORA
Peripatus

PYGNOGONIDA
Sea spiders

MYRIAPODA · MANDIBULATA · CHELICERATA · ARACHNIDA · ARANEAE · ARTHROPODA

Spiders (Araneae) fall between the whip scorpions (or whip spiders) and ricinuleids, which are thought to be their closest relatives. Whip spiders have three pairs of walking legs – the first pair being modified for use as feelers – strong pedipalps armed with spines, no venom glands, and they do not produce silk. Ricinuleids do not occur in southern Africa but are found in Central Africa and the American tropics. They are harmless, slow-moving creatures that live in leaf litter and probably feed on termites.

NAMING SPIDERS

Recognized common names exist for all spider families but not for all genera and species. Some common names, wandering spiders and orb-web spiders, for example, cover entire groups of spiders including unrelated families. These names may also vary from place to place and from language to language. For example, our button spiders are called widow spiders in America, and in South Africa many people refer to rain spiders as wolf spiders, and to solifuges (which are not spiders) as 'hunting spiders'. Using scientific names – although it might seem daunting and difficult at first – can eliminate confusion and enable arachnologists from Beijing, Buenos Aires, Berlin or Bloemfontein to discuss a specific organism without misunderstanding one another.

For clarity, scientific names are used throughout this book in conjunction with recognized common names. It is important to remember that groups or genera are constantly being revised, species shuffled from one genus or family to another, and new

8

species named as new research is undertaken. This is unavoidable since sorting and placing living things into groups is a dynamic process. The upsurge in molecular studies during the last few decades has also had a major impact on the classification of all living creatures, including spiders, and in many instances has revealed that organisms that appeared to be closely related are in fact not related at all and vice versa.

The binomial system of name-giving – a system through which all living things have been grouped in a logical way and given scientific names accordingly – was developed towards the end of the 18th century by Linnaeus. This system follows a strict code and, once this is understood,scientific names become much clearer and make more sense than any common name ever could.

Basically, the classification system always follows the same pattern: Take, for example, the classification of the yellow-and-black striped garden spider, *Argiope australis*.

Starting at the broadest category, it is a member of the animal **kingdom** (Animalia), the **phylum** Arthropoda (animals with jointed legs), and **subphylum** Chelicerata (animals with chelicerae and without antennae). The **class** to which spiders belong is Arachnida, which includes the orders to which spiders, scorpions, ticks, opiliones, mites, whip spiders, false scorpions and others belong. Within this class is the **order** Araneae (spiders), **suborder** Araneomorphae, **family** Araneidae, **subfamily** Argiopinae, **genus** *Argiope* sp. and, lastly, **species** *australis*. The generic name, *Argiope* sp., is something like the spider's surname, while the species name, *australis*, is its 'first name'. When only a generic name is used without the specific name, generic names are followed by the singular abbreviation 'sp.' or the plural 'spp.', for example *Argiope* sp.

Top: *Yellow-and-black striped garden spider,*
Argiope australis *(family Araneidae).*

SPIDERS' RELATIVES

What many people know as red roman spiders are not in fact spiders, although they are arachnids. They do not produce silk and have no venom glands. Other arachnids found in southern Africa include ticks and mites (Acari), whip spiders (Amblypygi), harvestmen (Opiliones), pseudoscorpions (Pseudoscorpiones) and

The red roman 'spider' is not really a spider.

Whip spider; also an arachnid, but not a spider.

Above: *Harvestman.*
Top: S*corpion with young.*

ABOUT THIS BOOK

The aim of this book is to introduce southern African spiders in an accessible way. Technical words for spider anatomy and behaviour have, therefore, been kept to a minimum and those that it has been necessary to use are explained in the glossary on pages 92–93.

In the first chapter we explore spiders' ancient roots, with an overview of spider evolution reaching back more than 300 million years, to a time when the earth was devoid of flowering plants and flying insects. The next chapter deals with the anatomy of spiders, familiarizing the reader with technical terms used in consecutive chapters. In Chapter 3 we discuss the unusual ways in which spiders perceive the world, and in Chapter 4 we explore the behaviour of these highly successful land predators, detailing their curious sex lives, their use of webs, and their special hunting techniques.

With almost 3 800 named species in 66 families occurring in the region, there are simply too many species to discuss in a book of this nature. Therefore, only the most commonly seen spiders and those of special interest have been selected, and are discussed in detail in chapters 5 and 6. The region's venomous spiders are discussed separately in Chapter 5. Chapter 6 is the field guide section of the book, and can be used to identify the family, genus or species of a spider according to its web type or habitat. Because quite closely related species do not necessarily look alike and can behave differently, and because many species are indistinguishable from one another with the naked eye, the spiders have not been grouped according to families or degrees of relatedness.

The spiders found in southern Africa belong to the order Araneae, and are divided into two suborders, the Mygalomorphae and the Araneomorphae (see diagram below). The Mygalomorphae are considered more primitive than the Araneomorphae, and there are only nine families belonging to this group in southern Africa, of which seven are discussed in this book. Members of 24 of the 54 Araneomorphae found in the region are discussed. The list of species is therefore by no means comprehensive, and you may well come across spiders that do not appear in this book. A list of all the spider families in southern Africa appears on page 91.

In the Appendix we discuss how spiders can be found, collected and photographed. If, as we hope, you feel inspired to make a serious study of spiders after reading this book, an excellent place to start is with Dippenaar-Schoeman and Jocqué's (1996) book, *African Spiders: An identification manual.*

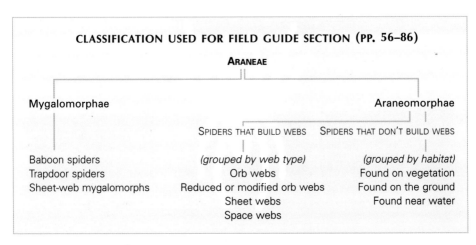

CLASSIFICATION USED FOR FIELD GUIDE SECTION (PP. 56–86)

ARANEAE

Mygalomorphae

Baboon spiders
Trapdoor spiders
Sheet-web mygalomorphs

Araneomorphae

SPIDERS THAT BUILD WEBS

(grouped by web type)
Orb webs
Reduced or modified orb webs
Sheet webs
Space webs

SPIDERS THAT DON'T BUILD WEBS

(grouped by habitat)
Found on vegetation
Found on the ground
Found near water

10

SPIDER EVOLUTION

*Spiders have been around far longer than most other land-living animals
and have outlived many life forms. Spiders first appear in the fossil record between
390 and 360 million years ago – before flowering plants or flying insects developed
and even before amphibians, which were very early colonizers of the land.*

Creatures called Trigonotarbida are among the oldest known fossils of land animals, dating back some 400 million years before the present. They were similar and quite closely related to spiders but lacked apparatus for spinning silk or producing venom. Spiders might have been around then too, but that is not known for a fact. The oldest officially recognized spider fossil dates from the late Devonian period, 374 million years ago. Known as *Attercopus fimbriunguis*, it was found to have spinning organs, which identified it positively as a spider. But the most ancient silk found so far dates from the Cretaceous period (60–130 million years before the present), preserved in Lebanese amber.

The oldest recorded spider fossil from South Africa was found in the Drakensberg and named Triassaraneus andersonorum. *Top:* Male sheet-web mygalomorph, Thelechoris sp. (family Dipluridae).

The history of spiders is intimately interwoven with the evolution of silk, its uses and, especially, the development of three-dimensional webs. It has been said that the evolution of spider silk was an evolutionary leap as important to spiders as flight was to birds, since it enabled them to modify their environment to accommodate their unique way of life. Webs were probably first developed during the Permian period (290–250 million years ago) when flying insects first appeared, although this has not been proven. We must assume that insect flight and spider webs evolved together: as insects developed flight to escape from ground-based predators, including spiders, spiders developed silken webs to snare their prey, which could now fly out of reach.

But *how* did spider webs evolve? It all happened so long ago and there is so little hard evidence that we can only make educated guesses. Webs might have developed from silken lines that radiated from the mouths of burrows or retreats, which these early spiders, like their modern counterparts, probably laid down as they moved around. These silken trails would have been similar to the slime trails of slugs and snails, and could have enabled them to find their way around and, because they probably contained pheromones, to recognize one another by scent. At the same time, they might have snared crawling insects and, as the millennia passed, the spiders with the most elaborate and efficient silk trails would have caught more insects, eaten better, bred more successfully and evolved increasingly more efficient webs. Spiders probably also started to produce silk to cover their eggs or to build retreats in which they could rest or hide.

The oldest recorded spider fossil from South Africa dates back to the Upper Triassic period, between 220 and 205 million years ago. It was discovered among plant and insect fossils found in the Molteno formation in the southern Drakensberg, and has only recently been described and officially named. It is known as *Triassaraneus andersonorum*.

A fossil of a more recent spider, dating back to between 95 and 65 million years before the present, was found at Orapa in Botswana. It looks modern and was probably a land-based hunting spider belonging to the superfamily Lycosoidea (a number of families found in southern Africa today belong to this superfamily), but because of the awkward way in which it lay in the sediment, with its head, eye pattern, chelicerae (fang bases) and copulatory organs hidden, further identification was not possible. This discovery is particularly valuable since it is the first spider fossil *described* from Africa.

All spider fossils are of great importance, because they are so very rare. Spiders did not fossilize well; their soft bodies decomposed fast, leaving little behind, and they often lived (and died) away from fossil-forming strata. However, enough fossils have been discovered through the years to start forming a picture of their evolution. Some fossils that are between 250–205 million years old belong to a spider family that is still around today, the Hexathelidae. Most hexathelids are found in Australia and

One of the most primitive among living spiders, an 'earth tiger' or liphistiid. Note the tough plates protecting the segmented abdomen.

New Zealand but there is also a species in the Mediterranean region and another in Cameroon, West Africa. The notoriously venomous Australian funnel-web spiders, *Atrax* spp., belong to this family. These spiders look very similar to fossilized spiders that are more than 200 million years old, and can be considered an important link between modern spiders and their prehistoric ancestors.

MESOTHELAE

Even more primitive among living spiders are those that belong to the suborder Mesothelae – a group of spiders that consists of only one family, the Liphistiidae or 'earth tigers', and includes 40 species. Liphistiids are restricted to parts of Southeast Asia, New Guinea and northern Australia. (They do not occur in Africa.) Unlike more modern spiders, which have two or three pairs of spinnerets and smooth, unsegmented abdomens, the Liphistiidae have a segmented abdomen and four pairs of spinnerets set far forward; each abdominal segment is protected dorsally by a tough plate called a tergite. Other characteristics, like the fangs opening parallel to the long axis of the body, can also be considered primitive. It is not always easy to distinguish accurately between primitive and modern characteristics – generally, if characteristics are more efficient they can be assumed to be a more recent development.

MYGALOMORPHAE AND ARANEOMORPHAE

The more modern spiders are set apart from their primitive relatives by their unsegmented abdomens and two or three pairs of spinnerets, which are usually set at the far end of the abdomen. They all belong to two suborders: the Mygalomorphae and Araneomorphae.

The **Mygalomorphae** do have some primitive characteristics, such as two pairs of booklungs, and fangs lying and articulating parallel to the long axis of the body (as in the Mesothelae) – but they lack other important primitive characteristics such as the segmented abdomen. They are much more

successful than the Mesothelae, being found on all continents except Antarctica. Southern African baboon spiders and trapdoor spiders, and the so-called bird-eating spiders and tarantulas from the Americas, all belong to this group.

A large black baboon spider, Harpactira *sp. (family Theraphosidae), a typical mygalomorph.*

Most mygalomorphs are robust, hairy spiders which live in burrows or silk-lined retreats. In southern Africa, they are generally found at ground level and quite a number construct trapdoors to their burrows. Tree trapdoor spiders, micromygalomorphs and sheet-web mygalomorphs live above the ground. Theraphosids from the rain forests in the tropics live and hunt in trees by night, and retreat to silk-lined hideaways in vegetation by day. Despite their formidable appearance and comparatively huge fangs, most are fairly harmless to humans. Their venom glands are usually quite small and lie inside the chelicerae (fang bases), whereas those of araneomorphs are comparatively large and are found inside the cephalothorax.

Most spiders belong to the suborder **Araneomorphae**. Araneomorphs are the most 'modern' or evolved spiders, and are distinguished from the Mygalomorphae by having only one pair of booklungs (or none at all), and fangs that articulate more or less at a right angle to the long axis of the body, and which open and close in a pinching motion (*see* diagram below). Araneomorphs are found in all imaginable habitats, whereas – in our region at least – most mygalomorphs are more restricted in their choice of habitat.

THE GREAT SURVIVORS

There is still much to learn about the evolution of spiders and it is entirely possible that more 'living fossils' will be discovered in future. However, what we do know for a fact is that, as a group, spiders are pretty successful – having been around, more or less unchanged, for millions of years. For this, in addition to the crucial role they play in keeping insect numbers in check, they deserve our respect. Therefore, next time you see a spider, don't just spray or squash it – stop and think. It might have come from an unbroken line stretching more than 370 million years into the ancient past. Rather spare it to become an ancestor of spiders of a few million years in the future. Spiders will probably be around long after we, and our kind, have disappeared from the face of this planet.

Argiope aurocincta (family Araneidae) has all the characteristics of a typical araneomorph.

DIFFERENCES BETWEEN THE MYGALOMORPHAE AND THE ARANEOMORPHAE

large fangs

2 pairs of booklungs

smaller fangs

1 pair of booklungs

Mygalomorph from below   *Fang from the side*   *Fangs from the front*   *Araneomorph from below*

A mygalomorph's fangs lie parallel to the long axis of its body, and therefore it has to raise its cephalothorax (head region) and strike downwards when it bites.

An araneomorph bites with a pinching movement, and its fangs open and close from the outside, inwards, more or less at right angles to the long axis of the body.

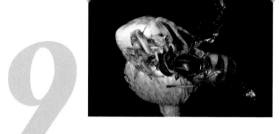

HOW SPIDERS FUNCTION

Spiders are very successful creatures – having been around, more or less unchanged, for hundreds of millions of years. They are among the most common land predators, and their bodies have been specially adapted to a predatory lifestyle.

Spiders are often mistakenly referred to as insects. In fact, they belong to a completely different group of arthropods, the Arachnida, and differ from insects in many ways. The most obvious difference is that they have two main body parts – cephalothorax and abdomen – whereas most insects have three main body parts: head, thorax and abdomen.

Spiders have eight legs (insects six), eight, six or two simple eyes (most insects have compound eyes), and no wings. They possess abdominal silk glands, and usually have three pairs of spinnerets from which the silk is extruded. Many insect larvae produce silk, but as a group they do not depend on it as much as spiders do. All spiders rely on silk to a greater or lesser degree for their way of life, and the ingenious ways in which they use it is one of their unique characteristics.

ANATOMY

To understand how spiders live and why they behave as they do, one needs to know something about their anatomy.

CEPHALOTHORAX

The cephalothorax is made up of the cephalic (head) and thoracic (thorax) regions; the upper plate covering the cephalothorax is known as the carapace. Although it is not always obvious that there are two regions, in some spiders there is a clear demarcating dorsal groove – called the cervical groove –

between them. Behind this groove there is a hollow called the fovea. Almost all spiders have a fovea, which serves as an attachment for internal muscles. The fovea can be longitudinal or transverse.

At the front of the cephalic region are the **eyes** in various configurations, usually in rows or groups. Sometimes the eyes are clustered together on one raised eye tubercle, sometimes on a ridge, on a keel or on separate protuberances. Most spiders have eight simple eyes, although some have six, or four, or only two, and some have none at all.

A male tropical wolf spider (family Ctenidae). These spiders have eight eyes grouped in three rows, with one pair being larger than the others. Top: *Flower crab spider,* Thomisus *sp., and prey.*

ANATOMY OF A SPIDER:
EXTERNAL BODY PARTS

MALE   FEMALE

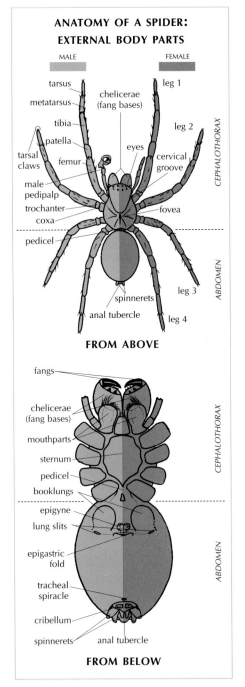

tarsus
metatarsus
tibia
patella
tarsal claws
femur
male pedipalp
trochanter
coxa
pedicel
chelicerae (fang bases)
leg 1
eyes
cervical groove
leg 2
fovea
CEPHALOTHORAX
pedicel
spinnerets
anal tubercle
leg 3
leg 4
ABDOMEN

FROM ABOVE

fangs
chelicerae (fang bases)
mouthparts
sternum
pedicel
booklungs
CEPHALOTHORAX
epigyne
lung slits
epigastric fold
tracheal spiracle
cribellum
spinnerets   anal tubercle
ABDOMEN

FROM BELOW

The cephalothorax houses the spider's **central nervous system**, which comprises two main, interconnected ganglia (encapsulated collection of nerve-cell bodies). The lower of these consists of the fused ganglia of the appendages, and links sensory information to movement. The upper ganglion is more or less equivalent to a 'brain'. This ganglion integrates visual information and probably also acts as a movement association centre.

At the front of the cephalothorax are the chelicerae (fang bases). Each fang base ends in a curved, moveable, hollow fang. There is a duct in each fang that leads to the **venom glands** situated inside the spider's cephalothorax. The venom glands are long, cylindrical organs attached to the fangs by the venom duct. The fangs are mainly used for injecting venom and digestive fluids into prey, but the chelicerae are also used for digging, carrying egg sacs or prey, and for defence.

A tropical wolf spider (family Ctenidae) has teeth on its fangs, which are used to crush its prey.

MOUTHPARTS FROM BELOW

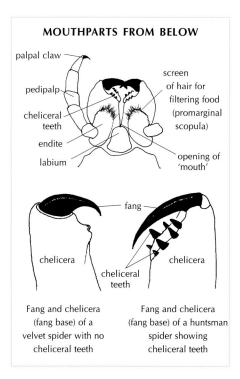

Fang and chelicera
(fang base) of a
velvet spider with no
cheliceral teeth

Fang and chelicera
(fang base) of a huntsman
spider showing
cheliceral teeth

teeth on their fangs only suck. Once the prey is immobilized, the spider vomits digestive fluid onto it, and then sucks up the resultant fluid through screens of hairs situated on the endites (*see* illustration, left), which filter out the solid bits. This process is repeated several times and initiates digestion outside the spider's body. Spiders with cheliceral teeth, plates or projections (*see* left) also crush and crunch their prey while it is being digested. After these spiders have finished their meal, only a tiny ball of hard parts is discarded. Spiders without cheliceral teeth simply suck the soft parts out of the prey and discard the empty outer skeleton in one piece.

Crab spiders (family Thomisidae) don't have teeth on their fangs; they feed by sucking body fluids from their prey.

On either side of the chelicerae (fang bases) are the **pedipalps**, resembling short legs. They have six segments, whereas legs have seven. In adult males the last segment of each of the pedipalps is modified as a copulatory organ, an unusual feature not found in other arthropods.

Four jointed **legs** are situated on either side of the cephalothorax. Most animals use flexor and extensor muscles to move their limbs, but spiders use hydraulics. Their haemolymph, or blood, acts as a hydraulic fluid and is pressurized and propelled into the limbs by strong muscles that are situated inside the cephalothorax.

Spiders that jump do not have enlarged legs like grasshoppers and crickets, but

A burrowing spider, Cydrela spinifrons *(family Zodariidae), showing the domed carapace typical of digging spiders.*

Spiders feed by sucking on their prey, and their **mouthparts** have been specially adapted for this purpose. Feeding techniques differ and are determined by the kind of mouthparts spiders have. Those with no

How spiders function

HOW SPIDERS CLIMB UP GLASS

Only certain spiders have the ability to climb up smooth surfaces. It all depends on whether a spider has pad-like tufts of hairs, called scopulae, on its tarsi (the 'feet', or final leg segments furthest from the body), or not. Spiders that live in webs or have evolved from web-living ancestors do not have these tufts of hair. But most hunting spiders, including wolf spiders, have scopulae. Under a high-powered microscope one can see how the tips of these hairs spread out like little brushes into thousands of fine 'end feet'. Each hair therefore has thousands of contact points with the substrate, and each foot has hundreds of thousands of contacts. Spiders can climb up smooth surfaces partly because most surfaces are not as smooth as they seem, and partly because most surfaces are covered with a thin layer of water. A mechanical force, known as capillary force, which is present when a solid comes into contact with a liquid, causes physical adhesion between the thousands of end feet and the smooth surface. If the film of water is absent, for example in the case of Teflon-coated surfaces, even spiders equipped with scopulae will slide.

Baboon spiders, jumping spiders and other spiders that rely on the strength of their legs to hold and subdue prey have even more of these hairs, and their scopulae often extend to the next leg segment, the metatarsus.

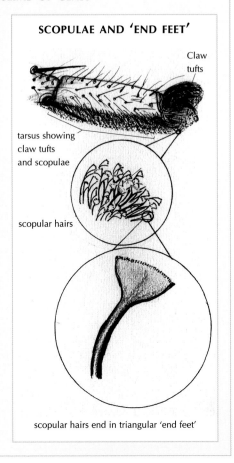

SCOPULAE AND 'END FEET'

Claw tufts

tarsus showing claw tufts and scopulae

scopular hairs

scopular hairs end in triangular 'end feet'

---

they do have high, domed carapaces to accommodate the muscles that power the haemolymph pressure. Lynx spiders (family Oxyopidae) are excellent examples of such spiders, and can leap long distances; so too, can many of the jumping spiders.

Digging spiders also need strong legs and have high carapaces. Very often the carapaces of adult male and female digging spiders do not have the same shape because the males are wanderers (they do not dig), while the females spend the greater part of their lives digging.

ABDOMEN

The abdomen is attached to the cephalothorax by a thin stalk called the **pedicel**, which, although very narrow, carries the aorta (major blood vessel), the intestine and the main abdominal nerve, all packed together with muscle and tendons.

The abdomen houses the digestive, respiratory and reproductive organs, as well as the heart and silk glands. The lung slits are the first set of openings situated on the underside of the abdomen, towards the front. The booklungs have a single opening

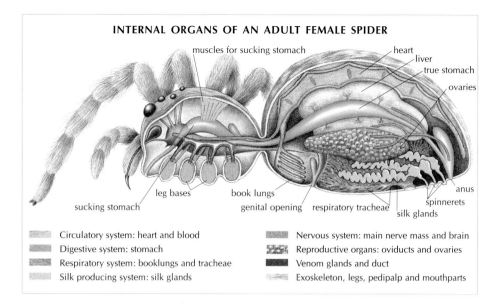

INTERNAL ORGANS OF AN ADULT FEMALE SPIDER

muscles for sucking stomach   heart
liver
true stomach
ovaries

sucking stomach   leg bases   book lungs   genital opening   respiratory tracheae   silk glands   anus   spinnerets

Circulatory system: heart and blood
Digestive system: stomach
Respiratory system: booklungs and tracheae
Silk producing system: silk glands

Nervous system: main nerve mass and brain
Reproductive organs: oviducts and ovaries
Venom glands and duct
Exoskeleton, legs, pedipalp and mouthparts

each, just forward and on each side of the epigastric fold (*see* page 16). The genital opening is located at the centre of the epigastric fold. The branched tracheae (*see* Respiration) are further back within the abdomen and usually have a single or sometimes two ventral openings, called spiracles, which can be located in various positions on the underside of the abdomen.

There can be as many as eight different kinds of silk gland, each producing a different kind of silk for a different purpose. Paired spinnerets (araneomorph spiders usually have three pairs and mygalomorph spiders two) are situated at the end of the abdomen, below the anus, and each spinneret terminates in a number of spigots. The spinnerets are well muscled, very flexible and can be moved independently of each other to place the silk exactly where it is needed. Certain spiders, called cribellate spiders, have an additional spinning organ called the cribellum. This can be a single plate or paired plates, thickly covered in thousands of tiny spigots which produce the extremely fine silk threads which join together to form the hackled bands of cribellate silk.

Spiders' abdomens can distend enormously, enabling them to carry their eggs and to gorge in times of plenty. This, together with their ability to fast during lean times by slowing their metabolic rate, is a very useful survival mechanism.

Respiration

Spiders have two kinds of respiratory systems: **booklungs**, which open on the underside of the abdomen, and one or two pairs of tubular **tracheae** or air tubes, which branch throughout the body and open to the outside through stigmata or spiracles. Most spiders have one pair of booklungs and tracheae, some have no lungs, only tracheae, and the mygalomorph spiders have two pairs of booklungs and no tracheae.

Booklungs consist of thin plates of permeable cuticle. Gas exchange takes place between the air on the one side of each plate and the haemolymph (or 'blood') on the other side. The tracheae lead air to various parts of the body, where gas exchange takes place through the thin walls at the ends of the tracheae. Spiders that spend time under water are covered with a thick layer of hairs.

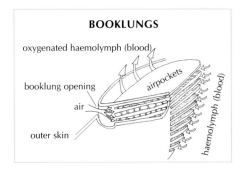

BOOKLUNGS

oxygenated haemolymph (blood)

booklung opening

airpockets

air

outer skin

haemolymph (blood)

These hairs can trap a bubble of air, acting as an external 'lung' that enables the spider to breathe under water.

Circulation

Spiders' **hearts** are long, muscular organs situated in the upper part of the abdomen, and stretch from the front end of the abdomen to the back. Unlike the blood of mammals, spiders' blood, or haemolymph, is clear. Although spiders have an open circulatory system, which means that the inside of their bodies is constantly bathed in haemolymph, they also have arteries leading the haemolymph away from the heart to the various parts of the body, including the booklungs. They lack veins to carry oxygen-poor haemolymph back to the heart — it is simply pulled back to the heart through the open body cavity as a result of the heart's pumping action. Non-return valves situated in the abdomen prevent back-flow.

Reproductive organs

The Araneomorphae are divided into two groups according to the complexity of their sexual organs. Those that possess simple copulatory organs, a feature that is considered primitive, are termed haplogyne spiders. Those with complex copulatory organs, a feature considered more 'modern', are termed entelegyne spiders.

The primary genital opening in both female and male spiders is situated on the underside of the abdomen between and slightly posterior to the booklungs in a fold called the epigastric fold. It is from this opening that males produce sperm and females produce eggs. In female spiders this opening leads to the internal reproductive organs.

The adult male's pedipalps are modified as copulatory organs, and usually have a conspicuous tibia and tarsus, specially adapted for the storage and transfer of sperm. (Females' and juveniles' pedipalps resemble short legs, don't have enlarged ends, and don't perform a sexual function.) As a male's pedipalps (located on the cephalothorax) are not directly connected to his genital opening, the sperm has to be transferred from the opening to the pedipalps, and from there to a female's genital opening. The male does this by depositing a drop of spermal fluid onto a small silken mat, known as a sperm web, and then sucking the fluid from the mat into his pedipalps.

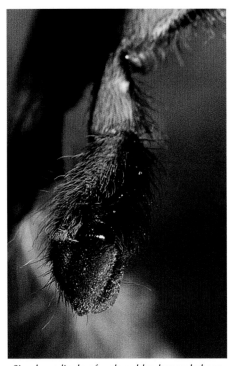

Simple pedipalp of male golden-brown baboon spider, Augacephalus *sp. (family Theraphosidae).*

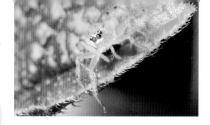

HOW SPIDERS PERCEIVE THEIR WORLD

Not only do spiders use their legs to move about, they also use them to produce sounds, to hear, and to explore their world through taste and smell. Most spiders rely primarily on their ability to 'taste-feel' to know what's happening around them, but spiders also have eyes and some have very keen vision.

SOUND-PRODUCING MECHANISMS

Spiders produce a variety of sounds, mainly to communicate with their own kind and to scare off predators. Many male spiders produce sounds to attract females during courtship or to intimidate rival males. These sounds are generally so soft that they are barely audible to the human ear. Sounds produced to scare off predators are much louder, and are produced by both males and females.

Spiders in different families or genera produce sounds in different ways. Scraper and file arrangements, found on opposing body parts, can be rubbed together to produce buzzing, clicking, hissing or purring sounds (*see* diagram, page 22) – this is called stridulation. Spiders can also produce sounds by vibrating certain body parts, or by drumming or tapping with their pedipalps, legs, or abdomens on natural objects like dry leaves, which act as amplifiers.

The males of certain wolf spiders produce hissing sounds by scraping the spiny bristles on the coxae (first joints) of their hindmost legs over the rough outer covering of their booklungs. Other wolf spiders have a file and scraper on the joint between the tibia and tarsus of the pedipalp (*see* page 22) which, when rubbed together, make a tiny rasping noise. Still others drum with their pedipalps or abdomens on the ground or any other substrate, or simply vibrate their legs or abdomens. In one species of spitting spider the male emits a soft buzz to attract females by rubbing together roughened areas on the outer side of its chelicerae (the file) and the inner side of its pedipalps (the scraper).

Baboon spiders, both males and females, hiss when alarmed, sounding much like snakes. While guaranteed to scare the living daylights out of a nervous arachnologist, the sound is not for use against people, but rather

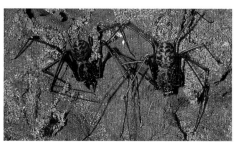

Spitting spiders, Scytodes *sp. (family Scytodidae), rub their chelicerae and pedipalps together to produce a soft buzz. Top: A jumping spider (family Salticidae, subfamily Lyssomaninae).*

SOUND-PRODUCING MECHANISMS

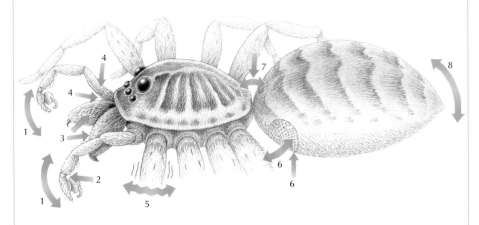

1. Using the pedipalps to drum on the substrate
2. Drumming produced at the joint between the tibia and tarsus of the pedipalp
3. Rubbing the insides of the fang bases together
4. Rubbing the pedipalp against the fang bases
5. Vibrating legs
6. Rubbing the fourth leg against the rough outer cover of the booklungs
7. Rubbing the spines on the back of the cephalothorax against a rippled area on the abdomen
8. Vibrating the abdomen.

as a defensive sound intended to deter small predatory animals. This is a much louder noise than the sounds used in spider-to-spider communication, and it is produced by rubbing together parts of the chelicerae (fang bases) and the pedipalps, which are covered with rough hairs.

HEARING

If spiders produce sounds then they must be able to 'hear'. Although they do not have external ears, as most mammals do, spiders have hearing organs in the form of various vibration receptors, which are very sensitive to vibrations in the air, on the substrate, in their webs and sometimes even on water. The most important receptors are hairs that cover the whole body, but which are concentrated on the limbs, especially the front ones. The most specialized hairs are trichobothria. These are much less common than ordinary tactile hairs, and are arranged in straight lines or small clusters on certain

WHY ARE SPIDERS SO HAIRY?

The different kinds of hairs found on spiders' bodies are used as sensory organs, and enable spiders to feel, hear and taste.

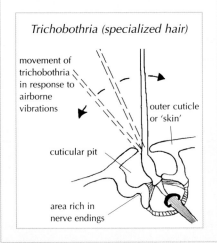

Trichobothria (specialized hair)

movement of trichobothria in response to airborne vibrations

outer cuticle or 'skin'

cuticular pit

area rich in nerve endings

Web spiders, like the black-and-yellow striped garden spider, Argiope australis *(family Araneidae), use their webs as expanded vibration receptors.*

leg segments. Trichobothria are suspended in a very thin cuticular membrane in small pits rich in nerve endings (*see* box, page 22). These very fine, long, flexible hairs are immensely sensitive to air currents and low-frequency, airborne vibrations. They move in response to these currents and vibrations, activating the nerves in the cuticular pits.

It may be difficult to think of hair as ears – but bear in mind that hair enables humans to hear. Hairs in the human inner ear move in response to airborne vibrations. These vibrations are passed on from the hair to tiny bones that cause the eardrum to vibrate, which in turn transmits this information to auditory nerves. These nerves send impulses to the brain where the sensory information is recorded as sound.

In addition to their hair, web spiders also use their webs as expanded vibration receptors. Even when spiders rest away from the web they will have at least one leg touching part of it, even if it is only one thread. Spiders are very skilled at distinguishing and interpreting any vibration or movement on the web, and know exactly which part of the web is being touched. Male web spiders rely on the female's ability to react to vibrations during the mating process, and court females by vibrating their webs.

Other organs sensitive to vibrations, gravity and the spider's own movements, are small, slit-like depressions or pits in the exoskeleton, known as slit-sense organs. When these organs are grouped together in waved, parallel patterns, they are called lyriform organs. Sensory information is transmitted through the thin 'floor' of the pits to nerve endings just below the cuticle. These slit-sense organs are found all over the spider's body, but are more numerous on the limbs.

SMELLING

Small, pit-shaped sensors, known as tarsal organs, are situated on the upper side of the tarsus of each front leg and the pedipalps. These organs are chemical (scent) receptors, or olfactory organs, which not only enable the spider to taste and smell, but also react to changes in humidity and temperature.

The adult female probably exudes a sex-specific substance (a sex pheromone) to attract males, and the male spider seems to be able to home in on the female from a considerable distance, even when she does not move. This seems to indicate that her scent is carried through the air and is picked up by males. Many male spiders also use this sense of 'taste by touch' to track down females of their species, when the latter have laid down scented silk trails.

TASTING

The spider's organs of taste are hollow 'taste hairs' that are open at the tips and are found mostly on the legs and palpal segments furthest from the body. An adult spider can have as many as a thousand of these chemosensitive hairs. You can test a spider's ability to taste by picking up a rain spider and watching it as it carefully taps with its long front legs on your hand, 'tasting' your skin and sweat. If you offer it a freshly killed insect it will 'taste' the insect first with the tips of its legs before accepting the offering. But if the insect has been dead for a long time, it will 'taste' it and then ignore it. If you put a bitter-tasting insect, for example a stink bug or a monarch butterfly, in a spider's web, it will taste the offering with its front legs, and then promptly cut it out of the web and drop it.

SEEING

Most spiders are nocturnal and rely primarily on their ability to 'taste-feel' to establish what is happening around them. Those that live in webs, whether diurnal or nocturnal, take their cues from the web itself. Considering this, one would think that web spiders, especially nocturnal ones, would hardly need to see. Nevertheless, they do have eyes and they do use them. Spiders that build webs every evening at dusk and take them down at dawn rely on their eyes, which are extremely sensitive to the quality of light, to tell them when to build or take down their webs.

There are some spiders (jumping spiders, family Salticidae, and wolf spiders, family

Above: *The pedipalps of the male* Portia *sp. (family Salticidae) are often decorated with thick brushes of hairs in contrasting colours.*
Top: *Ogre-faced spiders,* Deinopis *sp. (family Deinopidae), can see particularly well.*

Lycosidae, for example) with very acute vision, and if you look at them their prominent eyes are one of the first things you will notice. They have at least one pair of very large, forward-facing eyes situated at the front of the head, which can be compared to the telephoto lenses of a camera. The other six eyes can be compared to wide-angle lenses, and offer the spider a 360° wraparound view of the world. Certain jumping spiders reputedly have vision as keen, for their size, as that of birds of prey, but as most of them are diurnal their eyes are not designed for night vision.

Unlike jumping spiders, nocturnal wolf and ogre-faced spiders can see very well – even in the dimmest of lights. Wolf spiders, like many other hunting spiders, rely on vision not only to find and catch their prey but also to recognize and interact with others of their own kind. Male wolf spiders court females with elaborate waving and signalling of their front legs and pedipalps, which are often

conspicuously decorated. When the female sees this, she responds accordingly. The decorations of male jumping spiders are even more elaborate. Like wolf spiders, they also rely on the females' sense of vision to attract attention during courtship. With their energetic body posturing, waving pedipalps, often decorated with thick brushes of hairs in contrasting colours, male jumping spiders look very much like miniature drum majorettes! If you hold a mirror in front of a jumping spider, it usually notices its own reflection and will start signalling to the 'other spider', posturing and waving its pedipalps. Males often even attempt to fight their own image.

Wolf spiders (family Lycosidae) and funnel-web spiders (Agelenidae), can 'see' polarized light. Their eyes, therefore, play an important role in navigation. If you alter the polarization by holding a polarizing filter between the spider and the sun, the spider will set off in the wrong direction for home, and get lost.

4 SPIDER BEHAVIOUR

Spiders' success as predators can be attributed to the efficient ways in which they prey on other creatures, using webs to trap their prey, tracking their victims down on the ground, or simply waiting in ambush. Spiders' ingenuity is not restricted to their hunting techniques: one of their most interesting behavioural traits is the elaborate courtship rituals used during mating.

Most adult spiders are solitary and devote the greater part of their lives to catching prey, which can include prospective mates. This hostility towards members of their own kind is typical of most spiders. If you have ever tried to keep more than one spider in a container, you would have learnt how distinctly antisocial they can be. Should the opportunity arise, they tend to eat their

An enormous aggregation of Cyrtophora citricola webs on a river bank at Moremi, Botswana.
Top: *A pair of hammock-web spiders (family Linyphiidae) mating.*

mates, brothers, sisters, parents and young, leaving you with a single, fat, well-fed inmate. Not all spiders are antisocial, though. There are spiders that live in communities, the members of which not only tolerate one another but also cooperate and show a positive need for closeness.

The community web spiders, *Stegodyphus dumicola* and *S. mimosarum* (family Eresidae), are the only truly social spiders found in southern Africa. For a spider to qualify as 'social', all age groups and both sexes must live together, cooperate in prey capture and brood care, communicate, and show a need to be close to others of their own kind. Sociality among spiders seems to have evolved only where prey is continually abundant. For this reason, most social spiders are found in tropical latitudes and most, but not all, are web-builders. Some social spiders, like the African funnel-web spider *Agelena consociata* (family Agelenidae) from tropical West Africa, live in enormous colonies, sometimes consisting of more than a thousand individuals. Worldwide there are at least seven spider families with social species, and most of them live in webs. For a long time it was thought that spiders could not be social without webs, but it has now been discovered that although some spitting spiders (family Scytodidae) and an Australian huntsman spider, *Delena cancerides* (family Sparassidae), do not spin webs, they are truly social in every other way. *Delena cancerides* were used for the plague scenes in the film *Arachnophobia* because – being social – they can interact without eating one another.

Apart from the truly social spiders, there are also some species that are sometimes solitary and at other times communal. These 'in-between' spiders are solitary in their own webs but build their webs together in colonies with other spiders of their own kind. Tropical tent-web spiders, *Cyrtophora citricola*, for example, are sometimes solitary and at other times live in communities ranging from just a few to thousands of individuals, their webs grouped so closely together that they share scaffold lines. Individual webs built in communities are usually smaller than those of solitary spiders. Colonies of these 'in-between' spiders are normally established in places where there is an abundance of prey, for example, near an artificial light source or near water. Banded-legged golden orb-web spiders, *Nephila senegalensis*, and the related hermit spider, *Nephilengys cruentata* (family Tetragnathidae), sometimes build their webs so close together that they touch. Species of *Smeringopus* (daddy longlegs spiders) tolerate being very close to one another, and the young spiderlings often construct smaller webs within the space web of the mother.

The young of many spider species cluster together when they first emerge from the egg sac. During the summer, these 'lumps' of

Young fishing spiders of the genus Thalassius *(family Pisauridae) clustering together.*

Lycosa sp. (family Lycosidae) with young riding on her back.

spiderlings, often surrounded by a tangle of silk, can be found in most gardens. These are usually nursery-web spiderlings (family Pisauridae). If you blow on them they will move and stop collectively, resembling a school of fish. This synchronized movement is a protective device: one minute spiderling would be easy prey, but a bunch of little spiders, moving as one and looking like a creature a few centimetres wide, might cause small insectivores to think twice before attacking. Rain spiderlings cluster together for several weeks on the egg sac from which they emerged, and are guarded by the mother. After emerging, wolf spiderlings (Lycosidae) also stay together for a while, but unlike young rain spiders, they ride on their mother's back, clinging to her hairs.

Despite these examples of social behaviour, sociality among spiders is definitely the exception rather than the rule. Most spiders are asocial creatures that spend the greater part of their lives on their own.

COURTSHIP AND MATING

After their last moult most male spiders change their habits and become wanderers, concentrating on searching out and mating with females. When they find a suitable female, copulation takes place, often after an elaborate courtship ritual. During copulation the male first inserts one and then the other palpal organ into the female's genital

Unlike the male, the female buckspoor spider
Seothyra *sp. (family Eresidae), does not imitate*
other creatures.

The enormous female hermit spider,
Nephilengys cruentata *(family Tetragnathidae),*
(top) dwarfs the tiny male (bottom).

The male buckspoor spider, Seothyra *sp.*
(family Eresidae), imitates wingless wasps (also
known as velvet ants).

opening, thus transferring sperm from his pedipalps to her reproductive organs. After copulation, some male spiders, for example button spiders (*Latrodectus* spp.), leave a part of their palp in the female's genital opening as a kind of natural chastity belt.

The female genital opening and male pedipalp of spiders belonging to the same species are complimentary and fit into each other almost like a lock and key. Because each species' copulatory organs are unique, one of the most accurate ways of identifying adult spiders to species level, is to study their reproductive organs. Even though males and females of closely related species might, in theory, be able to copulate, they are prevented from doing so by the fact that they cannot understand the other's courtship rituals; as a result, the female will spurn the male's advances and will probably try to

eat him. Courtship rituals, therefore, not only appease the female by alerting her to a suitor's intentions, they also prevent hybridization with similar species.

Differences and similarities between males and females

Some male spiders are smaller than females, and can also look very different from the female. This is called sexual dimorphism and can be found in its most extreme form among some of the large diurnal orb weavers, such as those in the genera *Argiope* (family Araneidae) and *Nephila* (family Tetragnathidae), and also among flower crab spiders, *Thomisus* spp., and button spiders, *Latrodectus* spp. There are of course examples of spiders in which the male and female are more or less the same size: most wandering spiders – such as rain

The mating spur on the front leg of the male starburst baboon spider (Augacephalus sp., family Theraphosidae).

spiders in the genus *Palystes*, six-eyed sand spiders, *Sicarius* spp., and sac spiders, *Cheiracanthium* spp. – fall into this category.

Males are usually more slender than females, their legs are often longer, and they are fast and agile, features which can help them to escape predators, including, at times, their mates. They also mature earlier than their female siblings and therefore cannot mate with them. Mature males are usually more mobile than females and in some families can 'balloon' in the same way as spiderlings do (*see* page 45).

Some male buckspoor spiders, *Seothyra* spp., mimic ants or wingless wasps and move around above ground looking for prey and receptive females. The females of the same species do not imitate other creatures

Male and female Nemoscolus *sp. (family Araneidae) cohabit quite amicably.*

and never leave their burrows voluntarily. They are also larger, fatter, and less brightly coloured than the males.

Contrary to popular belief, male spiders are not often killed and eaten by females, but they do have to be careful. Besides the courtship rituals performed to avert this fate, certain physical attributes also act as safety mechanisms. Male baboon spiders are equipped with mating spurs, male water orb-web spiders, *Tetragnatha* spp., have elaborate chelicerae (fang bases), and some male jumping spiders have hooks and pegs on their chelicerae – all of which are used to hold the female or to immobilize her jaws.

Among the baboon spiders, adult males can be distinguished from females by the mating spur on the second joint of the front legs. This spur is hooked under the female's fangs during copulation, and serves the double purpose of pushing her back to expose her genital opening and of keeping her fangs out of the way, in case she accidentally uses them against her mate. Male baboon spiders are more or less the same size as females but have slimmer abdomens, longer legs and less vivid colours.

Courtship behaviour

When a male web spider approaches a female, he first tweaks and strums on her web to inform her of his presence and his intentions. He then carefully monitors her

Spider behaviour

reactions to determine whether they are positive or not. Sometimes she might react positively but at other times, when she is hostile towards him, he will only dare to approach her when she is preoccupied with prey. A male nursery-web spider, *Pisaura mirabilis*, from Europe does not live in a web, and appeases the female by presenting her with a 'peace offering'. This offering consists of an insect wrapped in silk. Only when the female starts eating the insect will the male approach her and start mating.

Male Australian red-back spiders, *Latrodectus hasselti*, which are related to our button spiders (family Theridiidae), seem to offer themselves to their mates' jaws as a kind of sexual sacrifice. After copulation has taken place, the male spider swivels around under the female so that his abdomen is right beneath her fangs. Sometimes the female eats the male, and sometimes she doesn't – there seems to be no definite pattern. This behaviour might ensure that the female gets enough protein to produce many healthy offspring that will carry the male's genes.

In some species of jumping spiders the male seeks out the female in her small, silken nest just before her final moult. When he finds her, he spins a nest nearby or right against hers, and waits until she has just shed her skin, rendering her too soft and weak to resist his advances. The males of some

The male garden orb-web spider, Argiope *sp. (family Araneidae), has complex copulatory organs and is a typical example of an entelegyne spider.*

A black button spider pair. The male (see arrow) is much smaller than the female. An egg case is visible behind the female.

crab spider species wait until the female is preoccupied with food before spinning fine strands of silk over her legs, creeping beneath her huge abdomen, and mating with her. The silken bonds cannot really hold the female but they do seem to quieten her. Other male crab spiders clamber onto the female's enormous abdomen, and then tap and stroke it to get her 'in the mood'. Only when she is sufficiently soothed will they clamber beneath her abdomen and mate. This foreplay is essential if the male crab spider is to survive – the female's genital opening seems dangerously close to her jaws!

Copulatory behaviour

In most cases males can just walk away after copulation but sometimes they have to beat a hasty retreat. Males tend to expend a lot of energy in finding females and during the mating process, and seldom eat during this time. As a result, they lose their vigour, their reactions slow down, and they become easy prey. If you look closely at adult male spiders, you will often notice missing legs. These limbs have probably been sacrificed in antagonistic encounters in a desperate attempt to survive. But not all males have to be wary of their mates. There are spider couples that cohabit amicably; male and female stone nest spiders, *Nemoscolus* spp., are often found together inside the central retreat.

Once male spiders have reached maturity and have mated with several females, they die. Females live longer than males because they must lay eggs, build egg sacs, and in some cases guard and protect their eggs and young. Long-lived spiders, such as female baboon spiders, experience many years of reproductive activity. Each time they moult, the lining of the reproductive organs is replaced and they become 'virgins' again, and need to be fertilized to lay fertile eggs.

EGGS AND SPIDERLINGS

In spiders with complex genitalia, fertilization does not take place at the time of mating. Sperm is stored in the female's body in a special chamber near the ovaries, called a seminal receptacle: the sperm is released only when the female lays her eggs. This process enables the female to lay several batches of eggs after just one mating. Spiders can lay anything from six to hundreds of eggs at a time, depending on the

The young of the banded-legged golden orb-web spider, Nephila senegalensis *(family Tetragnathidae), are not guarded or tended by their mother; the large numbers ensure that at least some survive to adulthood.*

Spider behaviour

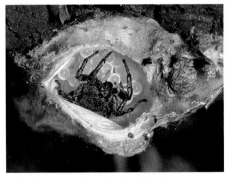

This jumping spider (family Salticidae) does not lay many eggs, and tends and guards her young.

species. Species in which females do not guard their eggs or young seem more likely to lay hundreds of eggs during their reproductive life span. Though mortality may be high among these spiderlings, the large numbers might ensure that at least some of the spiderlings escape predation, the vicissitudes of weather, and parasitism, to reach adulthood. On the other hand, spiders that guard their eggs possibly do not need to produce such large numbers of eggs. Their nurturing behaviour may protect the eggs and offspring against danger and ensure a proportionally higher survival rate.

Spiderlings hatch within the egg sac and moult once or twice before emerging from its silken safety. While they are still nourished by egg yolk their mouthparts and digestive systems are not completely formed and their spinning organs are not yet fully functional. Once the yolk is absorbed, they change skin again, and because their food source has dried up, many begin to show cannibalistic tendencies. To escape predation, the spiderlings start to disperse.

MOULTING

Spiders moult from five to about nine times before reaching adulthood, small spiders moulting fewer times than larger ones. They have to moult in order to grow, as the cuticle on the cephalothorax and limbs is hard and cannot stretch beyond a certain point.

The abdomen, however, is soft and can expand dramatically – as seen during times of plenty when spiders eat a lot.

One advantage of these skin changes is that lost limbs can be regenerated. If a spider loses a limb before reaching adulthood, the limb will gradually be regenerated after each moult until it looks just like the original, but if the spider loses a limb after reaching adulthood, the limb will not grow again, except among the Mygalomorphae and those spiders that continue to shed their skins after reaching adulthood. If the spider undergoes only one or maybe two moults after losing a limb, the limb will remain stunted. After suffering serious trauma, some spiders can detach the damaged limb at a weak point on certain joints, usually between the coxa and trochanter. This is done with a very fast, almost clicking motion, during which the thin membrane at the joint tears, causing the injured part of the leg to come off. The stump or remaining part of the leg usually seals fast and completely. Spiders often not only discard their injured limbs, they also eat them. Waste not, want not! Some spiders,

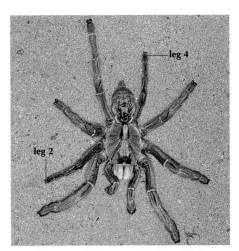

This horned baboon spider, Ceratogyrus bechuanicus, is regenerating two legs (see arrows). After the next moult, these legs may be full size again.

32

A nursery-web spider, Rothus sp. (family Pisauridae), shedding its skin. In the final picture a regenerated pedipalp (see arrow) is visible; it is still white and not quite complete.

Spider behaviour

flatties (family Selenopidae) for example, will voluntarily shed their legs to confuse predators in the same way lizards shed their tails. Spiders with less than the full complement of legs, or with legs that have not been fully regenerated, are fairly common, and they don't seem to be bothered by their 'handicap'.

FEEDING HABITS

Most spiders, both sedentary and wandering species, prey on a variety of invertebrates. Some spiders are 'generalists' and will capture and eat, within certain limits, whatever they can overpower; however, among web builders, the kind of prey taken is determined by the design and locality of the web. Other spiders are 'specialists', concentrating on specific prey items, and they come in many different guises. Some specialize in preying on ants, while others prefer termites. These spiders often live with these social insects, and some even mimic them. Certain specialists eat other spiders, while others like nothing better than spiders' eggs.

Since moths are common everywhere, one would think that they could be a ready food source for spiders, but most spiders find them difficult to catch as the wing scales come off easily, making them too slippery to handle. Hedgehog and bolas spiders (among others), however, have developed some particularly interesting techniques for catching moths (*see* page 68).

Fishing spiders, rain spiders and white lady spiders not only prey on insects but also on a variety of small invertebrates, while seashore spiders and intertidal spiders feed on crustaceans.

Termite-eating specialists

The family Ammoxenidae is endemic to southern Africa and includes two genera, *Ammoxenus* and *Rastellus*. Both are specialist termite predators. *Rastellus* spiders prey on termites In the genus *Psammotermes*,

---

HOW LONG DO SPIDERS LIVE?

The life span of different spiders varies dramatically: some spiders live only a few months while others survive for up to 20 years, but the majority live for one or two years. Longevity is not necessarily linked to size, and even big spiders, like the golden orb-web spiders, *Nephila* spp., and striped garden spiders, *Argiope* spp., live for less than a year. Many orb-web spiders (family Araneidae) live similarly short lives although it seems that tropical tent-web spiders, *Cyrtophora citricola*, live longer. Velvet spiders, *Gandanameno* spp., are also large and live for at least five years in captivity while their relatives, the community nest spiders, don't survive much longer than a year. Fishing spiders, *Thalassius* spp., live for a year or less, rain spiders, *Palystes* spp., for two or three years, and a captive six-eyed sand spider, *Sicarius* spp., has been recorded living more than eight years in captivity.

The longest-lived spiders may well be theraphosids (baboon spiders and tarantulas), which can live for more than 20 years in captivity. These long-lived spiders are always females since most male spiders have short lives – after reaching sexual maturity (sometimes within a year or two), they mate and die.

Ammoxenus amphalodes *(family Ammoxenidae) feeds on harvester termites,* Hodotermes mossambicus.

while sand-divers, *Ammoxenus* spp., feed on harvester termites (*Hodotermes mossambicus*), which are widespread throughout the region. Sand-divers can be found wherever their prey is active, and live in soil heaps at the mouths of harvester termite burrows. They also rest and bury their cup-shaped egg sacs in these soil heaps. Their chelicerae (fang bases) are modified for digging and, in action, they resemble miniature earth-moving machines. These spiders can move incredibly fast, and if disturbed, they will dive headfirst into the soil heaps, flip over onto their backs, and bury themselves.

Diores *sp. (family Zodariidae) in its igloo-shaped retreat.*

Ant-eating specialists

Diores spiders, one of the genera in the family Zodariidae, are specialist ant eaters. They live near ant colonies where they have easy access to their prey. They are small spiders and are usually yellowish-grey or light orange-grey in colour. They do not dig burrows but use silk and sand grains to build small retreats, resembling inverted 'igloos', on the undersides of stones.

Spider-eating spiders

Although most spiders make no distinction between spiders and other forms of prey and will catch and eat other spiders, should the

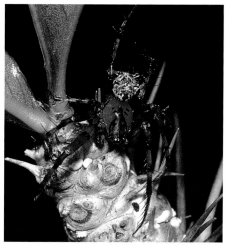

Pirate spiders, Mimetus *sp. (family Mimetidae), prey mostly on web-building spiders. They occasionally feed on free-ranging spiders.*

occasion arise, some specialize in feeding on their own kind. Pirate spiders (family Mimetidae) fall into this category and specialize in preying upon web-building spiders, and the occasional free-ranging spider. They are not very big (up to 7 mm), have an overall yellowish colour marked with dark blotches, and their front legs are armed with rake-like spines. They rely on stealth to trap their prey: first they invade the web of a potential victim and then they pluck and vibrate the silk, imitating a trapped insect or a courting male. This entices the owner of the web out of hiding, at which point the pirate spider will pin it down with the spines on its legs, and kill it with a fast-acting venom. Pirate spiders also feed on other spiders' eggs and on insects caught in their webs.

Dandy jumping spiders, *Portia* spp., are also spider-hunting specialists and their strategies, though similar to those of pirate spiders, are even more refined, versatile and sophisticated. 'Dandies' seem to 'play' their prey, fine-tuning their responses to make them do exactly what they, the predators, want. They can also adapt and change their methods of attack in response to different

Spider behaviour

Some spiders mimic ants, not necessarily to prey upon them but to gain the protection of numbers. Potential spider predators also tend to avoid ants because they bite, sting and swarm over their enemies. Some jumping spiders (genera *Myrmarachne* and *Cosmophasis*, family Salticidae) are among the most perfect ant mimics.

Jumping spiders, Myrmarachne *sp. (family Salticidae), mimic ants.*

An ant-like sac spider, Micaria *sp. (family Gnaphosidae).*

Above, left: *Members of the genus* Graptartia *(family Corinnidae) mimic wingless wasps in the family Mutillidae.* Above, right: *A jumping spider, genus* Cosmophasis *(family Salticidae), imitates the aggressive stance of* Camponotus *ants.*

There are ant-like sac spiders in the family Corinnidae and flat-bellied ground spiders (family Gnaphosidae) that mimic ants too.

Wingless wasps (family Mutillidae) are plentiful in some areas, have a painful sting and are likewise avoided by predators, so they too have their spider mimics – the male buck-spoor spider, *Seothyra schreineri* and *Graptartia* spp. (family Corinnidae), for example.

Some small orb-web spiders (family Araneidae), mimic small beetles and ladybirds.

The usefulness of these imitations is not immediately apparent but ladybirds, and probably beetles, are unpalatable and therefore unpopular with insect predators.

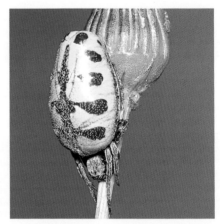

This spider, a member of the family Araneidae (species unknown), mimics a beetle.

A ladybird mimic, an unknown species belonging to the family Araneidae.

situations. Unlike pirate spiders that feed mostly on web-builders, dandy jumping spiders not only trick the occupants of webs by using vibratory signals, but also go on hunting forays to track down wandering spiders. Their acute eyesight enables them to outwit their more myopic prey.

SPIDERS' ENEMIES

Spiders have many natural enemies. Like insects, they are the major food source of a great number of larger animals: insectivorous birds make no distinction between spiders and insects; neither do lizards, chameleons, frogs, fish, shrews, bats, and others. Cannibalism among spiderlings, an extreme form of 'sibling rivalry', may also play a part in keeping spider numbers in check, as may spider-eating spiders such as the dandy jumping spiders, and the pirate spiders.

Spiders fall victim to various parasitic wasps. The smaller wasp species parasitize spider eggs, using their long ovipositors to deposit their egg or eggs on the host's eggs. The bigger wasp species lay eggs on living spiders: some of the very large wasps, for example *Pepsis* spp. (family Pompilidae), catch and paralyze baboon and rain spiders,

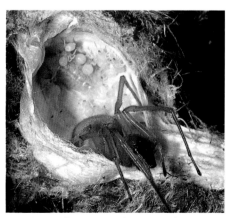

A wasp larva eating the young of a sac spider, Cheiracanthium *sp., (family Miturgidae). None of the spiderlings are likely to survive.*

and lay a single egg on each victim, then bury the spider and the egg, leaving the immobilized spider as a living larder for their larvae. In parts of America these wasps are called 'tarantula hawks'. It is fascinating to see how defenceless spiders seem to become when they are cornered by one of these wasps.

A large pompilid wasp, found in the Namib Desert, specializes in catching wheeling spiders in the genus *Carparachne*, and white lady spiders (genus *Leucorchestris*). As these spiders are nocturnal and the wasps diurnal, the wasps normally have to dig the spiders out of their burrows during the day. Sometimes, however, the wasp manages to track the spiders down when they venture out of their hiding places at dusk or dawn. To outwit the wasps, wheeling spiders have developed a unique means of escape, which is much faster and more energy efficient than running. When pompilid wasps detect them in the open, they flip over onto their sides, bend their legs, and cartwheel down a dune face on the leg joints between the tibia and the tarsus, at speeds of as much as a metre per second. When they reach the bottom of the dune they still need to run, but by that time the wasp may have lost sight of them.

Ichneumonid wasps simply lay their egg on a host spider, and then fly off. The unsuspecting host carries on as usual, while the larva feeds on it, and only expires when it has been sucked dry, and the larva is ready to pupate. Mud dauber wasps (family Sphecidae), each specializing in a different kind of spider or insect, stock their brood chambers with paralyzed prey. If you open these wasps' nests, you might find either green caterpillars, orb-web spiders or jumping spiders, depending on the wasp species.

Certain ground spiders, for example wolf and baboon spiders, often become infested with tiny, orange-red parasitic mites. These mites don't seem to harm the host spider but they may be an indication of poor condition, and are probably an irritant.

Spider behaviour

A pompilid wasp carries a paralyzed baboon spider, Pterinochilus *sp. (family Theraphosidae), to its burrow to feed its young.*

This false button spider, Steatoda *sp., will not live to adulthood. The ichneumonid wasp larva will eventually suck it dry.*

Apart from the external onslaught from predators and parasites, spiders also have to face a number of enemies from within. Deadly internal parasites, like roundworms or nematodes, enter the spider's abdomen while immature, and gradually start feeding on the host's digestive and reproductive organs. By the time the adult worm emerges, the host spider has been paralyzed and death soon follows.

Spider flies (Acroceridae) are another deadly internal parasite. The larva climbs up the host spider's legs, enters the booklung opening, and lives quietly between the lung plates. During the last stages of larval development, it leaves the lungs, enters the body cavity, and eats the spider's innards within the space of a few days. After the spider dies, the larva leaves the spider's dead body and pupates before emerging as an adult fly.

A male lesser baboon spider, Harpactirella *sp. (family Theraphosidae), infested with mites.*

A sac spider, Cheiracanthium *sp. (family Miturgidae), that has been killed by a parasitic spider fly larva (family Acroceridae). Note the spider's empty abdomen and the fly pupa (right).*

But of all spiders' enemies, humans and human activity probably pose the biggest threat. Blanket pesticides used in agriculture, horticulture and homes are the most dangerous. Pesticides eradicate prey and predators alike, often triggering worse pest infestations than the ones targeted. Ploughing lands for agriculture, building cities and towns, and altering the landscape for various other reasons cause havoc within many ecosystems, and can cause spiders, especially those that live in permanent burrows in the ground, to become locally extinct. The pet trade has also become a threat to certain spiders, especially the impressive ones like the baboon spiders. Populations in some areas have been decimated by indiscriminate collecting to satisfy the demand for spiders from collectors and fanciers, mostly from affluent countries in the northern hemisphere.

SILK – THE SPIDER'S ALL-PURPOSE TOOL

Spiders use silk in many ingenious ways: to modify habitats, to catch prey, and to protect themselves and their young. It is their ultimate weapon, their way of making their world spider-friendly. All spiders possess silk glands and spinnerets and use silk extensively, but not all spiders spin webs to catch prey.

The construction of webs is probably one of the most obvious uses of silk, but it is important to remember that there are more spiders that do *not* spin webs than ones that do. Although some hunting spiders do not build webs, the number and structure of certain body parts seems to indicate that some of these spiders evolved from web-building ancestors. The largest spider family, the jumping spiders (Salticidae), has very few web-building members. Some spider families consist of both web-builders and free-ranging hunters. Despite their common name, some orb-web spiders' webs (family Araneidae) – for example those of the African bolas spider, *Cladomelea akermani,* and the hedgehog spider, *Pycnacantha tribulus* – are so modified that they do not look like webs at all. Whether spiders build webs or not, most use silk to construct hiding and resting places. These can be temporary shelters, in which they can shed their skin, rest, or overwinter, or they can be permanent homes such as burrows, which may be constructed entirely from, or only lined with, silk. Trapdoor lids are also made of silk, which incorporates camouflage material from the surroundings. Silk is used to make egg sacs, and to convey signals during courtship. Furthermore, it is used by spiders as anchor lines, for swinging, for retracing their steps, for vibratory and chemical communication, and as a sensory extension of their own bodies. It is used for nurseries, fishing lines and as 'wings' (*see* page 45). Many spiders also wrap their prey in silk, and a number of them recycle silk by eating their webs when they take them down.

What is silk?

Silk is a fibrous proteinaceous substance that is 'manufactured' in special silk glands in the spider's abdomen. It leaves these glands as a water-soluble liquid and passes down progressively narrowing tubules to emerge as a solid thread from the spinnerets.

For a long time the process that causes the liquid to change to a solid thread was not fully understood. However, new research has shown that the protein goes through an 'acid bath' in the tubule (a similar process is used to manufacture rayon), which causes

Spider behaviour

A flat crab spider, Platythomisus sibayius *(family Thomisidae), 'sews' leaves together with silk to make a retreat.*

the liquid, water-soluble protein to become solid, waterproof silk as it moves from the silk glands to the spinnerets.

Spider silk does not consist of a single thread, which may seem to be the case when one looks at it with the naked eye, but is a composite of many threads. The strength and elasticity of the silk depends on various factors, one being the water content; a dry silk thread is more brittle and less elastic than one with a high water content. All spiders produce a variety of silks for different purposes. These silks are produced in different silk glands and emerge through different spinnerets.

Many of the orb-web weavers – such as the golden orb-web spiders (*Nephila* spp.), garden spiders (*Argiope* spp.), long-jawed water spiders (*Tetragnatha* spp.), field spiders (*Neoscona* spp.) and their relatives – construct orb webs which have droplets of adhesive on the catching lines. Other spiders, called cribellate spiders – feather-legged spiders (*Uloborus* spp., family Uloboridae) and certain hackled-meshweb weavers (family Amaurobiidae) for example – spin hackled silk to entangle their prey. A sieve-like spinning plate, called the cribellum, situated in front of the spinnerets, produces this silk, and a comb of modified hairs on the metatarsus of the fourth leg, called a calamistrum, is used to fluff the hundreds of strands into a hackled band.

WHY SPIDERS DON'T GET ENTANGLED IN THEIR WEBS

Most web-living spiders do not walk on their webs, but hang on them. (There are exceptions, such as the funnel-web spiders or Agelenidae, which walk on the upper surface of their webs.) The silk is held between the third claw and a set of stiff bristles on the spiders' feet or tarsi. To prevent the silk from sticking to the spiders legs, the tarsi are always kept scrupulously clean. Together, all these factors enable web-living spiders to move with ease in their webs without getting entangled or stuck.

Web-living spider's tarsus (above, left) *Tarsus with three claws and stiff bristles. When the spider moves in its web, the silk passes through these claws and bristles.*

Free-ranging spider's tarsus (above, right) *Tarsus with two claws and a claw tuft. The tuft enables free-ranging spiders to walk on smooth surfaces.*

Web types

Some spiders' webs are neither sticky nor fluffy, and therefore the owner has to rely heavily on its ability to sense vibrations in the web, and its quick response to these vibrations to catch prey before it escapes. In fact, webs act almost as an extension of the spider's body and can be used to assess very accurately the kind of prey that touched the web, its size and the exact place where it touched.

Tiny dew-drop spiders, Argyrodes *spp. (family Theridiidae), live as kleptoparasites in the webs of larger spiders – in this case, that of the golden orb-web spider.*

These spiders catch small prey that land in the web, help themselves to larger prey while the host spider is eating it, and sometimes even prey on the owner of the web and her consorts or young, should the opportunity arise. Some even eat the web itself!

Sometimes small flies share the spider's meal, feeding off the liquefying bits at the spider's mouth. Tiny spiders in the family Mysmenidae live as kleptoparasites, sharing a web with sheet-web mygalomorphs (family Dipluridae), and eating discarded morsels left by the larger spider.

The spider-hunting dandy jumping spider, *Portia* spp., is more ominous. It feeds on other spiders, their eggs and young. Community spiders' nests are sometimes invaded by moths (family Tineidae) that feed on the silk, ants that are attracted by food

Webs fall into three broad categories: orb webs, sheet webs and space webs. Within these there are endless variations, and webs differ not only from species to species, but also from one spider to the next within the same species. Individual spiders within the same species can adapt their webs, within certain parameters, to changing circumstances. With practice one can learn to identify spider families by their webs with a certain degree of accuracy. (*See* pages 42–43 for examples of certain web types.)

A web can lose its ability to snare prey over time. It can dry out, lose its stickiness, become dusty or get broken. For this reason, permanent webs need to be repaired from time to time. Permanent webs also attract predators like birds, bats, insects, parasitic wasps and spider-eating spiders. This is especially dangerous for spiders that remain in their webs all day. Some birds, for example bulbuls, sunbirds, tits and flycatchers, don't necessarily feed on spiders, but use their webs to build nests, often while the spiders are still in them.

Large, permanent webs are often invaded by kleptoparasites, of which dew-drop spiders, *Argyrodes* spp., are a common example.

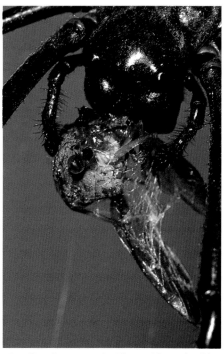

Tiny flies share a meal with a red-legged golden orb-web spider, Nephila inaurata *(family Tetragnathidae).*

Spider behaviour

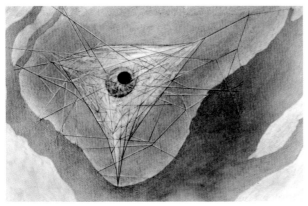 

Left: A space web (see page 73) built in the fork of a tree. This web is typical of members of the family Theridiidae, and has a rolled leaf at the centre, where the spider hides. **Right:** A ladder web built by a spider from New Guinea. Moths land at the top of the web, and tumble down to the bottom, losing their wing scales in the process, and eventually sticking fast.

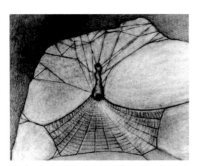 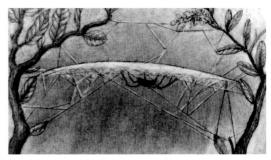

Left: A modified orb web with retreat built by Nemoscolus sp. (family Araneidae), see pages 67–69. **Right:** Hammock web of a spider in the family Linyphiidae, see photograph page 26.

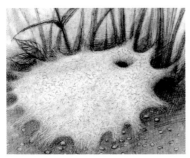 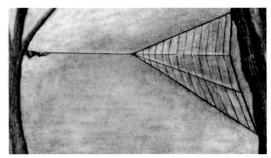

Left: A sheet web, see pages 70–72. **Right:** A triangle web, a variation of the classical orb web, belonging to Hyptiotes sp. (family Uloboridae), see pages 67–69.

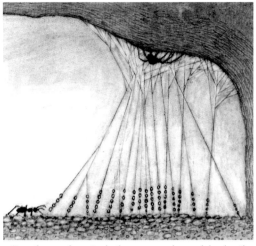

Gum-foot web typical of some members of the family
Theridiidae (see page 73). The vertical lines are sticky
at the base (hence 'gum foot') and are designed to
snare insects walking on the substrate.

Typical orb web of an araneid spider
(see pages 61–66).

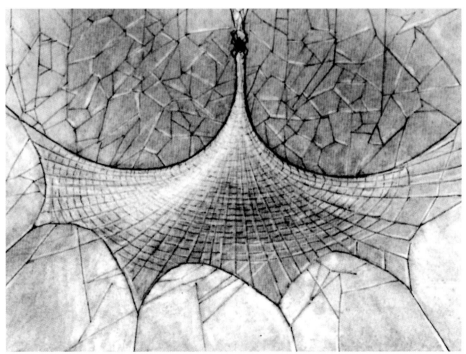

A tent web, another variation of the classical orb web, belonging to Cyrtophora citricola, see page 67.

Spider behaviour

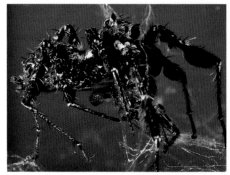

A dandy jumping spider, Portia sp. (family Salticidae), feeding on a theridiid spider.

A stone nest belonging to Nemoscolus sp. (family Araneidae).

remains but also feed on the inhabitants of the nest, and other spiders, notably Cheiracanthium spp. (family Miturgidae) and Zelotes spp. (family Gnaphosidae) that prey on the spiders themselves.

For the above reasons, spiders have to remove their webs from time to time and have to renew them often. Some webs are also built at dusk and removed at dawn to take advantage of the bounty of night-flying insects, and to avoid diurnal predators. To save valuable protein, many spiders eat their webs when they take them down. These spiders hide away during the day.

Other spiders construct a retreat off the web and hide there while monitoring vibrations on the web from a distance. Many orb-web spiders (family Araneidae) spin a single line from the hub of the web to their retreat, which constantly keeps them in touch with movements on the web. Should you see a web with no spider in it but a dry leaf or piece of debris hanging in it,

Achaearanea globispira (Theridiidae) constructs its home with sand grains bound in silk.

don't be fooled. The leaf or the piece of debris might well be the owner's hiding place or even the owner itself, pretending to be a leaf!

Stone nest spiders, Nemoscolus spp., construct retreats at the centre of their orb webs using tough silk into which they weave grains of sand or pieces of vegetation.

Certain cobweb spiders (family Theridiidae), such as *Achaearanea* spp. and *Theridion* spp., build similar retreats. An elaborate home is constructed by the bauble spider, *Achaearanea globispira*. This spider's retreat (or 'bauble') is suspended by a single thread below a rock overhang; it is made of silk and small pebbles, and has a silk spiral passageway inside. Below the retreat is a gum-footed web, which consists of non-sticky threads radiating down- and outwards from the bottom of the retreat. The 'feet' or ends of the threads are sticky and trap insects on the ground, hence the name of the web.

Spider silk is impregnated with the scent of the spider that spins it, and drag lines can leave information for other spiders of the same species long after their creator has passed. One of the ways in which males of both web-building and wandering spiders can find potential mates is to follow these scented, silken lines.

Flying spiders

Silk allows certain spiders to travel in a unique and interesting way, known as aerial dispersal or 'ballooning'. Silk strands emitted from the spider's spinnerets are suspended by air currents, enabling the spider to float through the air. Spiders 'balloon' by attaching silk threads to the substrate, walking a distance to extend the silken lines, and while doing so, extending their legs and lifting their abdomens until the breeze lifts the silk enough to carry the spider and the silk away. A weak spot in the threads, usually close to where they are attached to the substrate, causes the threads to break when enough has been extruded. For a long time it was thought that only small and young spiders could disperse in this way, but research has shown that adult males and even females with a body weight of up to 100 mg can balloon.

Spiders probably disperse because of overcrowding, which leads to local food shortages. Dispersal could also be triggered by external environmental factors, a specific time of year, or a particular stage in the spider's life cycle. This behaviour enables spiders to utilize all available habitats, and helps spiderlings to escape the cannibalistic tendencies of their siblings. Spiders are sometimes not carried very far by air currents, and many may land in unsuitable places, but there are always enough survivors to colonize new sites. On rare occasions spiders are carried along by very strong air currents and can cover enormous distances. This is one of the reasons why spiders, like flying animals, are often among the first colonizers of newly formed oceanic islands. There have even been reports of spiders that were collected in nets attached to weather balloons, far above the surface of the earth.

A flat-bellied ground spider, Micaria *sp. (family Gnaphosidae) preparing to balloon by letting fine strands out of its spinnerets.*

Spider behaviour

5 DANGEROUS SPIDERS

Worldwide only a handful of spiders are known to harm people, and few deaths directly attributable to spider bites have ever been reliably recorded. Spiders are reluctant to bite, and defensive bites against large mammals, including humans, are the exception and not the rule.

Spiders are a group of actively venomous animals. Their venom is a cocktail of different proteins, primarily designed to paralyze or kill their prey, which is usually insects. Of all the spiders found in the region, only the Uloboridae don't produce venom; all the other spider families have paired venom glands.

We do not know much about the effect of the venom of the vast majority of spiders because they seldom come into contact with people. Size and colour have nothing to do with how venomous a spider is. Only about 20 to 30 species of the thousands of spiders

found throughout the world are known to be of medical importance to man, and of those spiders only a tiny proportion have been known to kill humans. The majority of small spiders are incapable of penetrating our comparatively thick skins. In fact, if you take the higher number of 30 known venomous species and divide it by a conservative 30 000 (the number of known spider species in the world), it leaves you with a mere 0,01 per cent of known spiders that can be considered dangerous! But if you take the extrapolated probable number of spider species at 150 000, it comes to even less than 0,002 per cent! Statistically, you are as likely to be killed by a venomous spider as you are to live to 120 years of age.

THE FEAR OF SPIDERS

Bearing the above figures in mind, it is difficult to understand why spiders cause such universal fear and revulsion. Looking at the facts, there seems to be no good reason for people to assume that spiders are dangerous and 'out to get them'. From a rational point of view, it would be much more sensible to be afraid of elephants, cars or ticks. Perhaps it is because spiders are an unknown quantity, or perhaps it is the way they can suddenly and silently appear out of nowhere; perhaps their webs put people off or perhaps it's all those legs? It might even be the hair, but then why do people like stroking furry mammals?

Spiders, like exotically colourful silver marsh spiders, should not be feared but rather appreciated for their beauty.
Top: *A female Karoo button spider,* Latrodectus karrooenis *(family Theridiidae).*

Despite its fearsome looks, a big-eyed jumping spider (family Salticidae) can be most appealing.

Maybe it has something to do with people's perception of beauty. When you put your preconceived ideas about spiders aside and look objectively at a horned baboon spider, for example, you cannot but appreciate its beauty. The same can be said for the exotically colourful silver marsh spiders, and few creatures are as cheekily enchanting as an inquisitive, big-eyed jumping spider.

Perhaps the fear of spiders is as ancient as humankind itself. If you live close to nature and habitually sleep on the ground, as our distant ancestors did, it pays to be wary of little creatures with potentially painful bites or stings. To protect their offspring, sensible mothers would have passed on this wariness to their children who, in turn, passed it on to theirs. In this way the fear could have been reinforced from generation to generation. On the other hand, perhaps the opposite is true: modern humans are so far removed from the natural world, and our homes and even our gardens are often kept so ridiculously insect- and spider-free, that we have forgotten how to coexist with other creatures. We should guard against our own selfishness, and learn

to make allowances for creatures, including spiders, to investigate our homes. Spiders should be considered allies, not enemies.

In some cases, however, the fear of spiders is not unfounded. In Australia, for example, species of the venomous mygalomorphs, funnel-web spiders (*Atrax* spp., family Hexathelidae), are a real problem. These spiders are distributed widely across Australia and are common in some densely populated areas, which means that they regularly come into contact with people. Unusually, the male is the problem because in his search for females he sometimes comes indoors and so into contact with people. The Sydney funnel-web spider, *Atrax robustus*, is common in and around Australia's largest city. This highly venomous spider is fast and when cornered, reacts aggressively. Until recently, a number of people died from *Atrax* spp. envenomation because the treatment was symptomatic and not always effective. But today there is an antivenin available which, if administered correctly and in time, can save lives. A strange fact about *Atrax* spp. venom is that while it has a virulent and sometimes lethal

Dangerous spiders

A female daddy longlegs spider, Smeringopus sp. (family Pholcidae), carrying her egg sacs in her jaws.

There is a worldwide urban legend that daddy longlegs spiders are incredibly venomous, probably the most venomous in the world. Perhaps this legend has its roots in ignorance, but more likely it is a case of mistaken identity. Although daddy longlegs spiders are completely harmless, they can be confused with the dangerous violin spider, because the two species are superficially similar. Like daddy longlegs spiders, spitting spiders (*Scytodes* spp.) and false violin spiders (*Drysmusa* spp.) are harmless, but can also be mistaken for violin spiders.

A female spitting spider, Scytodes sp. (family Scytodidae), with an egg sac in her jaws.

A false violin spider, Drymusa sp. (family Drymusidae).

Spitting spiders make useful house mates and should be welcomed into your home; they do not build unsightly webs, only hunt by night, and they prey on ants, fish moths and smaller spiders. They also don't bite people. False violin spiders and true violin spiders look very similar but the former live in webs (most true violin spiders don't have webs). False violin spiders are nocturnal and are restricted to forested areas, caves and overhangs in the Western Cape – it is therefore unlikely that you will ever see one unless you look for it very carefully.

Legends aside, the male of the Sydney funnel-web spider, *Atrax robustus*, from Australia, is probably the most venomous spider in the world. An expert on these spiders, Dr Raven, warns: "... it really doesn't matter much which one (of the various species), if you get bitten by a funnel-web when you're on your own, my advice is to make peace with God first, then put on a pressure bandage and get to a hospital".

effect on primates, including people, it has no impact on dogs, cats, rabbits and Australia's small, predatory marsupials.

In South America, wandering spiders in the genus *Phoneutria* (family Ctenidae) are also rightly feared. They are large, aggressive hunting spiders, come indoors frequently, and their bites are apparently excruciatingly painful and can result in death from kidney failure. Wandering spiders belonging to the same family are found in southern Africa too, but there have been no reports of bites.

In the last few decades it has become fashionable, especially in the northern hemisphere, to keep tarantulas and baboon spiders as pets. Despite their fearsome looks, they have relatively small venom glands and their bites are painful mainly because their fangs are long (up to 10 mm), strong, very sharp, and can penetrate deeply.

A female horned baboon spider, Ceratogyrus brachycephalus *(family Theraphosidae), in aggressive pose.*

Even though our baboon spiders are said to be more aggressive than the rather placid American tarantulas, their bites, though painful, do not have lasting ill effects on people. Lesser baboon spiders, *Harpactirella lightfooti*, may have a venom more potent to man than that of the larger species, but this has not been proven satisfactorily.

Pterinochilus murinus, found in East and south east Africa, inflicts a very painful bite but has no dangerous systemic effects on people, while an arboreal baboon spider from West Africa in the genus *Stromatopelma*, may have a dangerous bite. The Indian ornamental baboon spiders, *Poecilotheria* spp., are also arboreal and have a venom that causes very painful and unpleasant reactions in humans. These spiders are beautiful and are much sought after by 'spider fanciers' but they are undeniably aggressive and accidents do happen. In South Africa, however, it is illegal to import, trade in or keep exotic (foreign) arachnids, including tarantulas, and in most provinces a permit issued by Nature Conservation is needed to capture, transport and keep our local baboon spiders.

INNOCENT 'MONSTERS'

Rain spiders, *Palystes* spp., are feared because of their impressive size, but are, in fact, not dangerous. Fifteen species have been recorded from our region, the most common and widespread being the big, grey-fawn *Palystes superciliosus* and the similar-looking *P. castaneus*. The latter occurs in and around Cape Town and along the southern coastal belt. Both can cause quite a stir when they come indoors, which is quite unintentional since they're simply looking for insects that are attracted by lights. If handled, they *can* bite and their fangs easily puncture human skin, but the symptoms of their bites are mild – a slight itching and swelling which may last a day or two.

Rain spiders, Palystes *spp., are feared because of their impressive size, but are in fact harmless.*

Dangerous spiders

SPIDER BITES

If you do get bitten by a spider, don't assume that your general practitioner or pharmacist knows much about spider bites. Experience has shown that the majority of diagnosed 'spider bites' are usually quite unrelated clinical conditions. Antibiotics, which can be expensive, are often prescribed as a matter of course, but are sometimes unnecessary and generally useless because they're intendedfor bacterial infections, and not for spider bites. However, infected wounds can sometimes develop into rapidly spreading inflammation of body tissue, which requires aggressive antibiotic therapy.

There is only one way to diagnose a spider bite accurately, and that is to catch the spider in the act. But this is almost impossible when the initial bites are not felt as in those spiders with cytotoxic (cell destroying) venom. Therefore, if you get bitten, try to collect the spider responsible, even if it is squashed, and take it with you when you seek treatment. Your medical professional can then have the animal identified, and administer the correct treatment.

As far as first aid is concerned, antihistamine ointments and pills are useful, and topical anaesthetic ointments or even old-fashioned calamine lotion can alleviate itching. An inexpensive and useful first aid treatment for any arthropod bite or sting (including spider bites) is immediate immersion in very hot water, which may neutralize the venom. This does not always work but is worth trying.

SPIDERS OF MEDICAL IMPORTANCE

The only dangerously venomous spiders in southern Africa are button spiders, some of the sac spiders, violin spiders, and maybe six-eyed sand spiders, but none of these have been known to kill people. It must be remembered that not all mammals react in the same way to a specific venom. For example, it was found that cows are very sensitive to the venom of certain widow spiders, and can die from a bite; humans are

also affected by it but less severely, while other mammals such as dogs, sheep and rodents, hardly show any reaction. In the same way, the venom of six-eyed sand spiders, *Sicarius* spp., kills laboratory rodents, but we don't know what the effect of their bites would be on humans. Even if their venom could kill humans, these spiders are generally found in inhospitably hot, arid regions with sparse human populations and are, therefore, seldom encountered.

CAN SPIDERS SPIT?

Yes, spitting spiders, *Scytodes* spp. (family Scytodidae), spit a mixture of gluey silk and venom from their fangs. The gluey silk pins the prey down, while the venom paralyzes it. These are the only spiders known to produce silk from the front part of their bodies, and a careful look at the spider will show that the cephalothorax is very high and domed to accommodate the strong muscles used to pressurize the gluey mixture which they spit.

As with poisonous mushrooms and venomous snakes, you should familiarize yourself with spiders that can cause harm, and learn to avoid them. (A good place to start is to study the detailed accounts of venomous spiders on pages 51–55.) But not only venomous spiders should be left alone; most spiders can administer bites and should be treated with respect. There have been occasional reports of adverse reactions to bites from a nocturnal orb-web field spider, *Pararaneus* sp., a palp-footed spider, *Ikuma* sp., a flattie, *Anyphops* sp., a rain spider, *Palystes superciliosus* and a jumping spider (family Salticidae). However, the effect of the bites of the majority of spiders on warm-blooded animals, including humans, is seldom severe. Most spider bites cause only local swelling and itching, which subside after a while although people can sometimes react badly for no apparent reason.

Violin Spiders

Family Sicariidae
Subfamily Loxoscelinae
Loxosceles spp.

Web: None. Sometimes a few strands of bluish silk are laid down.

Venom: Mainly cytotoxic (cell destroying), but it also has some haemotoxic elements which affect the blood. Bites can be serious and can cause extensive scarring, but no deaths have been recorded. Their fangs are short, so that bite wounds are tiny and superficial. Violin spiders are nocturnal and usually bite people while they sleep, so bites are often not noticed immediately. After about two hours, swelling starts and a dark area appears at the site of the bite. Over the next few days swelling increases, and a dark-coloured area appears along with blistering. This subsides and sloughs off

Violin spider, Loxosceles *sp. (family Sicariidae).*

around the fourth day, and could leave a deep, ulcerating wound that can spread dramatically and may take a long time to heal. Secondary infection may develop causing extensive tissue loss. There are unconfirmed reports of the symptoms of the venom 'travelling' and ulcerations appearing elsewhere on the body.

Distribution: Throughout southern Africa. Occurs naturally in caves and has extended its range over the years, via mines, to built-up areas. Occasionally wanders into houses in parts of Johannesburg, where it is infrequently found in dark corners. The majority of other species occur in savanna regions and are commonly found under rocks, logs and tree bark, or in old termite nests and rubble. These species seldom venture indoors.

Description: 8–19 mm. Yellowish or reddish-brown with a vague violin-shaped marking on the carapace. Six eyes and slender legs. Wandering, nocturnal hunters.

First aid and treatment: If a violin spider bite is suspected seek medical attention. The lesion should be kept covered and clean; cutting out of damaged tissue should be avoided. Treatment is supportive and symptomatic to limit infection. Oral and topical analgesics can be administered for pain and if infection sets in, aggressive antibiotic treatment (intravenous not oral) should be administered under medical supervision. FOLLOW-UP TREATMENT ONCE A DAY is highly recommended.

Violin spider, Loxosceles *sp. (family Sicariidae).*

Dangerous spiders

Sac Spiders

Family Miturgidae
Cheiracanthium furculatum and other
Cheiracanthium species

Web: None. Temporary sac-like, silken retreats in which they rest during the day, built in, for example, leaves, folds of material and in the corners of rooms.

Venom: These spiders are possibly responsible for 75 per cent of recorded spider bites in the Gauteng area, and probably throughout southern Africa. Initially the bite is not painful and often people do not notice that they have been bitten. As the fangs are large and the chelicerae (fang bases) can be opened very wide, two separate puncture marks are often visible. The venom is cytotoxic (cell destroying). The site of the bite becomes swollen, red and itchy. After a while a painful, unsightly boil-like sore develops which can ooze puss, and takes about a fortnight to heal. Occasionally symptoms similar to those of tick-bite fever develop. However, the incubation period is different to that of tickbite fever, and starts two to three days after the bite. As with all fevers, the symptoms are unpleasant, but will pass without treatment.

The sac spider, C. furculatum, *is responsible for 75 per cent of recorded spider bites in Gauteng.*

Distribution: Throughout southern Africa.

Description: 8–12 mm. Pale, cream-coloured spiders with a darker, leaf-shaped marking on the top of the abdomen. The legs are long, and the 'face', including the chelicerae (fang bases), are very dark. These spiders often venture indoors to hunt, and are common in many of our most densely populated regions. They are fast-moving spiders, with large fangs for their size, and will bite readily if squashed in clothing against the skin. Because they often rest in the folds of curtains, bed sheets, clothes, washing or bath towels, human/spider contact is common. Remember always to check your towels before drying yourself.

First aid and treatment: There is no particular first aid or medical treatment. Keep the bite site clean and covered to prevent secondary infection. Headaches resulting from the fever may be treated with analgesic.

Six-eyed Sand Spiders

Family Sicariidae
Subfamily Sicariinae
Sicarius spp.

Web: None

Venom: We don't know how dangerous the venom of these spiders is or even if it is dangerous to man, as no case studies are known. However, laboratory rodents have shown massive tissue damage and some have died as a result of envenomation. This does not prove that they are dangerous to humans, but it probably pays to be wary.

Distribution: Throughout southern Africa in dry, hot and sandy areas. It is a good idea to examine the ground and remove spiders (and scorpions!) if you are going to sleep outdoors in such places.

Description: 8–19 mm. Crab-like with long, strong legs, a broad carapace and a slightly rectangular abdomen. General colour brown, but tufts of hair trap and hold sand so that the spiders take on the colour of the ground in which they live. They mostly lie still, just below the surface. If unearthed, they can run

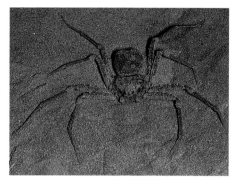

The six-eyed sand spider, Sicarius *sp., may be dangerously venomous.*

fast but will bury themselves again as soon as possible by using their legs to throw sand over their bodies. They are fairly long-lived, have a very low metabolic rate, do not need to eat often, and can stay immobile for weeks or even months at a time.

Button Spiders (Widow Spiders)

Family Theridiidae
Latrodectus spp.

There are six button spider species in the region: four black and two brown ones.
Web: Irregular space webs of very strong, elastic silk. The different species have slightly different web designs, built at different heights from the ground, and they can all adapt their designs to the physical circumstances in which they find themselves. A retreat of thick, opaque silk is attached to one side of the web, and can incorporate leaves, sticks, small stones, sand or prey remains.
Venom: The venom of the western black button spider, *Latrodectus indistinctus*, has been found to be three to four times as virulent as that of the common brown button spider, *L. geometricus*. Although they are feared for their venomous bites, it is difficult to think of button spiders as dangerous because they are not aggressive. When threatened, they normally hide away in the thick silk retreats at the side of their webs. If their webs are broken they will fall to the ground with legs curled around their bodies and feign death, apparently hoping that the threat will disappear so that they can return to their web in peace. It is only when they are accidentally trapped against the skin, or if they mistake some part of the human body for prey, that they will bite. But bites seldom occur: button spider silk is extremely strong and you feel it long before you reach the spider, or it reaches you. Their habit of wrapping prey in silk before administering a bite also ensures that a human finger, for example, is unlikely to be mistaken for prey – you'd definitely notice being wrapped! Male button spiders are small, and although their venom is probably as potent as that of females, there have never been reports of bites from male button spiders.

Female black button spider, L. renivulvatus, *with egg sacs.*

Symptoms: Mortality resulting from the bite of widow spiders is less than one per cent, worldwide. To date there have been no reliable reports of deaths in South Africa. Untreated, symptoms from bites last for about five days and are really unpleasant; complete recovery may take weeks. Initially the site of the bite is painful, but in some instances it may not be felt. After about 10 minutes to an hour the pain spreads to the lymph nodes closest to the bite site, from where it spreads to the muscles and joints. Strong, painful muscle cramps develop and the abdominal muscles become rigid (this is an important diagnostic feature). The face becomes contorted, flushed and sweaty, and the eyelids swollen, lips inflamed and jaw muscles contracted. A toxin in the venom can pass the blood/brain barrier and attack the central nervous system, resulting in severe psychological symptoms ranging from anxiety to absolute terror.

A dark-coloured female brown button spider, L. geometricus, wraps a beetle in silk.

A light-coloured female brown button spider, L. geometricus, with typical spiky egg sacs.

Distribution: Black button spiders: *Latrodectus cinctus* is widespread in the eastern parts of Africa. In the southern African region it is found from Cape Town along the south coast to the eastern and central parts of the region. *L. indistinctus* occurs along the south-western and north-western Cape coast and into Namibia, as far north as Swakopmund. *L. karrooensis* is found in the Karoo region, and *L. renivulvatus* throughout central southern Africa.

Brown button spiders: A cosmopolitan species probably spread around the world by man, *L. geometricus* is found from temperate to tropical countries throughout the world. It is also found throughout southern Africa. *L. rhodesiensis* occurs in Namibia, Botswana, Zimbabwe and the northern parts of South Africa.

Description: 8–20 mm. Males 2,5–6,5 mm. Abdomen globular; legs long and slender. Black button spiders have variable red, creamy and yellow markings on the dorsal side of the abdomen. Immature spiders, and occasionally adults, have a dull red marking on

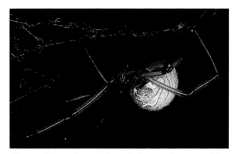

A very light-coloured female brown button spider, L. geometricus.

the underside of the abdomen. Young spiders and males often have red and creamy stripes across the dorsal side of the abdomen.

The colours of brown button spiders range from creamy white and gold, through to various browns, and very dark brown and black. There is a bright red or orange marking under the abdomen, more or less the shape of two isosceles triangles set apex to apex.

Button spider egg sacs have distinctive shapes, textures and colours. Those belonging to black button spiders are smooth, cream coloured, usually spherical, and about the size of a green pea. Brown button spiders' egg cases are spherical, cream coloured, roughly the size of a green pea, and

covered in small spikes. Rhodesian button spiders have fluffy, greyish or cream coloured egg cases, which are at least double the size of those of the other species.

First aid and treatment: Keep the patient still, quiet and warm. Reassure him or her that medical treatment will offer relief within less than half an hour. Get the patient to a medical professional as soon as possible.

The amount of venom injected is minute and acts quite slowly. The patient is definitely not going to fall down dead on the spot and there is ample time to get to a doctor. However, button spider bites should be considered serious and medical attention must be sought. The patient must also be kept under observation for a few days. Sometimes no symptoms occur at all; whether this is because the bites are 'dry' or whether the individual bitten does not react, cannot be determined. If no adverse reactions occur, no treatment should be given. Recognized treatment involves the injection of antivenin intravenously. The antivenin binds to the toxins, and the patient starts to feel better within 10–20 minutes. The antivenin treatment should only be administered in a hospital by a qualified medical professional.

Rhodesian button spider, L. rhodesiensis, with large, fluffy egg sacs that are diagnostic of this species.

Dangerous spiders

IDENTIFYING SPIDERS

This is not a comprehensive guide to southern African spiders, but a collection of the most commonly seen and most interesting spiders of the region. In an effort to make the list more complete, photographs of related spiders appear below spider accounts, where appropriate. The naming of spiders has been kept as simple as possible, and most accounts are to genus level, unless the spider can be identified to species level with the naked eye – in these cases representative species are discussed. A number of the accounts are at family level.

Southern African spiders fall into two main categories: Mygalomorphae and Araneomorphae (*see* page 10). For the purposes of this book the Araneomorphae spiders are discussed under the following headings: spiders that build webs (orb webs; reduced or modified orb webs; sheet webs, and space webs); and spiders that don't build webs (spiders found on vegetation; ground spiders and spiders that live near water).

Top: *Hedgehog spider,* Pycnacantha tribulus.

These categories are not absolute: spiders wander and are not necessarily restricted to one habitat. Especially in the larger families, there are representatives that occur in a wide variety of habitats. To get a more realistic picture of all the places where spiders can be found, refer to the list on pages 87–88 in conjunction with this chapter.

Note: Measurements are taken from the front of the chelicerae (fang bases) to the end of the abdomen and *exclude* the legs.

COLOUR GUIDE TO ARANEOMORPH SPIDERS

Spiders that build webs

Orb webs

Reduced or modified orb webs

Sheet webs

Space webs

Spiders that don't build webs

Spiders found on vegetation

Ground spiders

Spiders that live near water

Mygalomorphae

These are mostly robust, hairy spiders which usually live in burrows or silk-lined retreats (some construct trapdoor lids to their retreats). In southern Africa most burrow in the ground, with the exception of the tree trapdoor spiders and sheet-web mygalomorphs, which live above ground, and the micromygalomorphs (family Microstigmatidae), which are found in the undergrowth of humid forests. See page 14 for the main characteristics that differentiate mygalomorphs from araneomorphs.

Baboon Spiders

Family Theraphosidae

Web: None. They live in silk-lined burrows (without lids) in the ground, in natural crevices or in hollows under rocks and logs, etc. Males wander and construct temporary silken retreats to rest in during the day.

Venom: Not known to be harmful to man. Bites are painful due to size and depth of punctures from the huge fangs, up to 10 mm. In most cases the venom is mild. The effects of bites from the lesser baboon spider, *Harpactirella lightfooti*, may be more severe.

Distribution: The family Theraphosidae has a pantropical distribution with the subfamily Harpactirinae widespread in southern Africa. Genera found in southern Africa are: *Augacephalus* (starburst baboon spider), *Brachionopus* (lesser baboon spider), *Ceratogyrus* (horned baboon spider), *Pterinochilus* (golden-brown baboon spider), *Harpactira* (common baboon spider), *Harpactirella* (lesser baboon spider), *Idiothele* and *Trichognatha.*

Malelane golden-brown baboon spider, Augacephalus breyeri.

Male Namaqua baboon spider, Harpactira namaquensis, inspecting a female's burrow.

Description: 13–60 mm. Heavily built and hairy with robust legs and long, leg-like pedipalps. Four booklungs. Small eyes clustered together on a single tubercle towards front of carapace. Spinnerets protrude beyond end of abdomen. Adult males have smaller abdomens and a mating spur on the first pair of legs. Baboon spiders are nocturnal hunters, but can remain underground for weeks. On reaching adulthood, the males wander in search of females.

Horned baboon spider, Ceratogyrus brachycephalus.

Identifying spiders

Sheet-web Mygalomorphs

Family Dipluridae

Web: Three-dimensional sheet web of fine silk in various layers, interconnected with tunnels, leading to a retreat built amongst rocks, tree trunks, or banks. The webs stay in place for years and therefore play host to many other small creatures (insects and spiders) – some of them living as parasites, klepto parasites, and some as predators on the host spider and its young.

Venom: Not known to be harmful to man.

Distribution: This family occurs throughout the region. Two genera occur in southern Africa, *Thelechoris* and *Allothele*.

Description: 5–22 mm. Hairy, dark grey-brown with paired pale spots on the abdomen. Lightly built compared to other mygalomorphs, with a flat carapace and a pair of very long spinnerets. The eyes are grouped together on a tubercle towards the front of the carapace. These spiders lurk in tunnels in their webs and only run out to catch prey when it lands on the web. Adult males leave their webs to wander in search of females.

Above: *Sheet-web mygalomorphs (family Dipluridae) are more slender than most other mygalomorphs.*

TRAPDOOR SPIDERS

Web: None. Live in silk-lined burrows closed with trapdoors.

Venom: Not known to be harmful to man.

Distribution: Throughout southern Africa.

Description: Recognizable by their burrow-lids – if you can spot them! Females seldom venture from their burrows; they wait to ambush prey from below the partly opened lid. After their last moult, adult males wander in search of females. They have longer legs and slimmer abdomens than the females, and may have different colouring.

SOUTH AFRICA'S RAREST SPIDER

In 1917 African purse-web spiders, *Calommata simoni* (family Atypidae), were collected near Pretoria; they were not seen again in South Africa until 2003. They are, however, still fairly common in the rest of Africa and they have been observed living in large colonies in West and Central Africa.

The female seals herself inside her burrow and does not leave it even to look for food. She kills her prey by spearing it with her immensely long fangs through the wall of her catching chamber, and then drags it into her burrow through slits in the silk – which explains why *C. simoni* is extremely difficult to find. These reclusive spiders were thought to be locally extinct until a survey carried out in a nature reserve in Gauteng Province turned up a lone male almost a century since the last recorded collection.

Web: None. Lives in a silk-lined burrow in the ground, with a crater-shaped ambush chamber at ground level camouflaged with soil.

Venom: Not known to be harmful to man.

Distribution: Reported from West, Central and southern Africa, but may be more common and widespread.

Description: 9–30 mm. The front part of the carapace is high and the chelicerae (fang bases) massive with very long fangs. The legs are short and stubby with the first pair being very tiny. Apparently this spider has a pronounced manure-like smell, probably to attract flies. This species is the only member of the family Atypidae found on the African continent.

Cork-lid Trapdoor Spiders

Family Ctenizidae
Stasimopus spp.

Only one genus, *Stasimopus*, found in the southern African region.

Description: 15–43 mm. Dark and robust with short, stout legs and a domed carapace. Eyes in two rows towards front of carapace. Legs and abdomen hairy but the cephalothorax is shiny with few hairs. Burrow has thick, tight-fitting, cork-like lid.

Cork-lid trapdoor spider, Stasimopus *sp.*

Wafer-lid trapdoor spider, Ancylotrypa *sp., and burrow.*

Wafer-lid Trapdoor Spiders

Family Cyrtaucheniidae
Ancylotrypa spp. and *Homostola* spp.

Description: 9–32 mm. Front legs shorter and thicker than fourth pair of legs. Domed carapace with eyes in rectangular group towards front of carapace. Burrows built in open ground, in leaf litter, under logs, etc. Burrows can be complex, with more than one opening, or simple, with a single opening; some have side burrows while others consist of only one burrow. Lids are wafer-like flaps. Some burrow walls extend like a cuff above the soil surface.

Spurred Trapdoor Spiders

Family Idiopidae, subfamily Idiopinae
Genolophus spp., *Galeosoma* spp., *Gorgyrella* spp., *Heligmomerus* spp., *Idiops* spp., *Segregara* spp.

Description: 8–33 mm. Domed carapace with six eyes towards front of head and one pair far forward. Burrow lids either cork- or wafer-like. Apart from these lids, some genera such as *Galeosoma*, also have a second line of defence: when the burrow entrance is breached by an enemy, they plug the entrance with their armoured abdomens.

Hard-bum spurred trapdoor spider, Galeosoma *sp. (Family Idiopidae).*

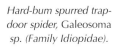

Trapdoor, Banded-legged Trapdoor and Tree Trapdoor Spiders

Family Migidae
Poecilomigas spp. (Banded-legged) and *Moggridgea* spp.

Banded-legged trapdoor spiders, *Poecilomigas* spp., build bag-like silken retreats in crevices in the bark of living trees.

Poecilomigas sp. (family Migidae) and burrow. Note striped legs.

Moggridgea spp. build similar retreats in hollows and in crevices on the ground or on or under rocks or tree trunks. Retreats are camouflaged with pieces of bark, lichen or moss. Some construct a single trapdoor at one end of the retreat, while others build two – one at each end. *Moggridgea* spp. are found in the eastern parts of southern Africa.

Tube trapdoor or Wishbone trapdoor Spiders
Family Nemesiidae

Description: 13–30 mm. Carapace low. Eyes on a well-defined, raised tubercle. Silk-lined burrows do not always have a trapdoor; some are open. Burrows vary from single to Y-shaped, and to ones with separate arms.

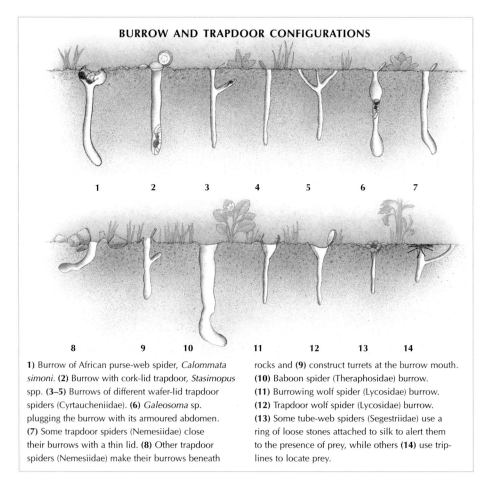

BURROW AND TRAPDOOR CONFIGURATIONS

1   2   3   4   5   6   7

8   9   10   11   12   13   14

1) Burrow of African purse-web spider, *Calommata simoni*. (2) Burrow with cork-lid trapdoor, *Stasimopus* spp. (3–5) Burrows of different wafer-lid trapdoor spiders (Cyrtaucheniidae). (6) *Galeosoma* sp. plugging the burrow with its armoured abdomen. (7) Some trapdoor spiders (Nemesiidae) close their burrows with a thin lid. (8) Other trapdoor spiders (Nemesiidae) make their burrows beneath rocks and (9) construct turrets at the burrow mouth. (10) Baboon spider (Theraphosidae) burrow. (11) Burrowing wolf spider (Lycosidae) burrow. (12) Trapdoor wolf spider (Lycosidae) burrow. (13) Some tube-web spiders (Segestriidae) use a ring of loose stones attached to silk to alert them to the presence of prey, while others (14) use trip-lines to locate prey.

Araneomorphae

Also called 'true' spiders, these spiders are found in all imaginable habitats while the Mygalomorphae, in our region at least, are generally restricted to burrows in the ground. With tens, if not hundreds of thousands of species in 91 families throughout the world, the Araneomorphae come in an incredible variety of shapes and sizes, and differ from one another in almost every possible way, including distribution, habitat, longevity and web type (or complete lack of it).

SPIDERS THAT BUILD WEBS

ORB WEBS

These webs have a typical 'wagon wheel' design, can be vertically, obliquely or horizontally inclined, and are mainly one-dimensional (*see* page 43). The most common orb-web spiders are those belonging to the families Araneidae, Tetragnathidae and Uloboridae. Orb webs vary in terms of design, and if differences such as orientation, spacing of spirals and radii, web decorations, stabilimenta (*see* page 62), trip-lines, retreats and web placement are taken into account, one could say that each species' web is unique.

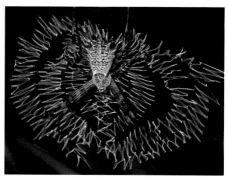

Juvenile garden orb-web spider, Argiope flavipalpis, *with disc-shaped stabilimentum.*

Adult female banded garden orb-web spider, Argiope trifasciata.

Adult female garden orb-web spider, A. flavipalpis, *with cross-shaped stabilimentum.*

Identifying spiders

FAMILY ARANEIDAE

Garden Orb-web Spiders

Subfamily Argiopinae
Black-and-yellow Garden Spider
Argiope australis

Female Argiope australis *(bottom), with the tiny male (top).*

Web: An orb web made of strong yellowish silk and set low on vegetation with sticky capture threads. No retreat. Stabilimentum across centre of web vary from web to web, from day to day and at different stages in the spider's life cycle. The web is more or less permanent but is sometimes deserted by the spider if a site becomes untenable if, for example, the web is constantly broken by traffic or if there is a shortage of food in a specific area.

Venom: Not known to be harmful to man.

Distribution: Widespread throughout region.

Description: Females up to 24 mm, males around 5 mm. Lobed abdomen with yellow and black dorsal stripes. Colouring varies from bright yellow and black stripes to creamy yellow and grey. The cephalothorax is silvery and the legs banded in black and yellow; the third pair of legs is shorter than the others. Males are often seen on the adult female's web. Prey consists of flying and jumping insects. When the prey lands in the web, the spider tugs at the silk strands to ascertain where the prey is, rushes to touch-taste and feel it, manipulates it and then wraps it in silk. One can see the spinnerets working and thick loops of silk being thrown around the prey as it is twirled around. Only when the prey is completely immobilized with silk does the spider bite to paralyze it. Adults are seen throughout the region during the summer months.

STABILIMENTA

Stabilimenta are zigzags of loosely woven, white silk radiating from the hubs of webs, and are considered a 'trade mark' of the garden orb-web spiders, although other diurnal orb-web spiders construct them too. Their consistency differs considerably from that of the rest of the web (the catching or structural silk), and they take on a variety of forms. They can differ from one species to the next, between different individuals of the same species, and also at different stages in the spider's life cycle or under different external conditions, such as food abundance and climate. They can be cross-shaped, single oblique lines, vertical or horizontal lines or even elaborate discs. Spiders that construct a stabilimentum usually remain out on the web during the day and at night, and without a stabilimentum to hide behind they would be vulnerable to predators and parasites. The stabilimentum breaks up the spider's outline, making the owner of the web more difficult to detect, but also makes the web more visible, thus preventing larger animals from breaking it unintentionally.

Other theories regarding the function of stabilimenta have also been put forward: for example, that they adjust web tension, lure pollinating insects by mimicking the ultraviolet reflective patterns that some flowers use to attract insects, or that they are simply there to strengthen the web. It is possible that they might fulfil all of these functions.

Orb-web Spiders

Subfamily Araneinae
Araneus spp., *Neoscona* spp. and *Pararaneus* spp.

Araneinae is one of the largest subfamilies in the enormous family Araneidae.

Web: Orb webs. Sizes and details of design vary according to species.

Venom: Not known to be harmful to man but

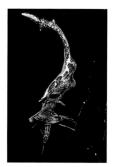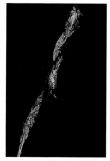

Orb-web spiders (from left to right): *Female scorpion-tailed spider,* Arachnura *sp.; female garbage-line spider,* Cyclosa *sp.; female* Poltys furcifer; *and female bright green* Araneus apricus.

there are occasional anecdotal reports of bites inflicted by *Pararaneus* spp. causing neurotoxic envenomation.

Distribution: Widespread throughout region.
Description: *Araneus* spp. 5–12 mm, *Neoscona* spp. 5–17 mm and *Pararaneus* spp. 15–20 mm. Males of most nocturnal species not much smaller than females but males of some day-active species can be much smaller. Most are fawn, yellow, brown, grey or green; some are plain coloured while others have patterned abdomens. Abdomens overhang the cephalothorax and come in a variety of shapes, but are mostly oval with a narrow rear and wide front.

Araneus spp. and *Pararaneus* spp. hide in retreats constructed of silk and surrounding vegetation, to the side of the web. They monitor what goes on in the web by holding on to a silken thread attached to the web hub. *Neoscona* sit head-down at the centre of the web. After prey is caught, it is wrapped in silk. Many araneids are nocturnal, spinning their webs in the evening and removing them again at dawn.

Female orb-web spider, Neoscona *sp.*

Bark Spider

Caerostris sexcuspidata

Web: Large, classical orb web with close spirals.
Venom: Not known to be harmful to man.
Distribution: Widespread throughout region.
Description: 8–22 mm. Male much smaller than female. Abdomens vary considerably within the species, some have twin projections, some only one and others just tubercles which resemble thorns, knot holes, broken twigs, etc. Colours of spider imitate those of bark and lichen. When in the web, the spider positions itself head-down at the hub. Mostly nocturnal, taking its web down at dawn. During the day it sits motionless with its legs pulled up neatly against its sides on the bark of a tree, where it is almost invisible due to its cryptic coloration and strangely-shaped abdomen.

Bark spiders, Caerostris sexcuspidata, *showing the strangely-shaped abdomens.*

Identifying spiders

Yellow-and-black Kite Spider

Subfamily Gasteracanthinae
Gasteracantha versicolor

Web: Classical orb web, often several metres above the ground, with closely placed radii and an open hub.
Venom: Not known to be harmful to man.
Distribution: Common and widespread.
Description: Female about 8 mm, with abdomen overhanging the cephalothorax. The cephalothorax is hard and shiny, and yellow in colour with black markings and thorny projections. Legs short. The spider sits head-down at the hub of the web during the day. Male much smaller and less brightly coloured than female and lacks thorny projections.

Female Gasteracantha versicolor.

Female Gasteracantha
milvoides.

Female Isoxya
tabulata.

Female Gasteracantha sanguinolenta.

FAMILY TETRAGNATHIDAE

Banded-legged Nephila

Subfamily Nephilinae
Golden orb-web spiders
Nephila senegalensis

Web: Enormous orb web of strong golden silk. Spiral capture threads sticky and closely spaced. Web is left in one place for a long time; gets repaired when it gets broken or becomes dusty and loses its stickiness. Young spider builds complete orb, but as the spider matures the web appears to become misshapen with the hub migrating upwards toward the bridge line. The web is protected by a barrier web at the back and front, and a vertical line of prey remains is often left hanging among the trip-lines.
Venom: Not known to be harmful to man.
Distribution: Widespread throughout region.
Description: The female is very large (25–30 mm) has a cylindrical abdomen, and black-and-yellow banded legs; the third pair is much shorter than the others. Cephalothorax silvery, abdomen black marked with yellow. Patterns and colour intensity vary. This spider

Huge female banded-legged golden orb-web spider, Nephila senegalensis, *and tiny male.*

Female hermit spider, Nephilengys cruentata. *This spider's silk is white, not golden like that of other members of subfamily Nephilinae. Distribution cosmopolitan.*

Left: *Female and male black-legged golden orb-web spiders,* Nephila pilipes. *Small male is feeding on female's prey.* Right: *Female red-legged golden orb-web spider,* N. madagascariensis.

can be found singly or massed together in such large numbers that their webs overlap one another. Female usually shares her web with several males. Male much smaller than female and can weigh up to a thousand times less. Males may vary in size from individual to individual.

Female lays up to a thousand eggs, and can produce up to four egg sacs. If one looks carefully at the web of *N. senegalensis,* one

will probably also find tiny metallic-coloured dew-drop spiders (*Argyrodes* spp.) living as kleptoparasites in the larger spider's web. *Nephila* spp. normally go unnoticed until they reach their full size from midsummer onwards. During this time their large webs, and the females' impressive body size, often draw attention. These spiders are sometimes referred to as golden orb-web spiders because most of them produce golden silk.

Long-jawed Water Orb-web Spiders

Subfamily Tetragnathinae
Tetragnatha spp.

Web: An orb web with an open hub, more or less horizontal, in vegetation near or over water.
Venom: Not known to be harmful to man.
Distribution: Widespread throughout the region with some cosmopolitan species.
Description: 6–15 mm. Males similar in size to females. Fawn, creamy, yellowish and light brown with long, cylindrical bodies, pointed towards the rear, and long, slender legs. They have very long chelicerae (fang bases) and because the males' pedipalps extend beyond the fang bases, males appear to have four 'jaws'. *Tetragnatha* spp. usually hang under the open hub of their webs near or over fresh water, with two pairs of legs stretched forwards and two backwards. They are generally active during the night. These spiders erect their webs at dusk and can be watched while doing so, but if

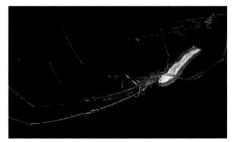

Female long-jawed water orb-web spider, Tetragnatha sp. (subfamily Tetragnathinae).

Identifying spiders

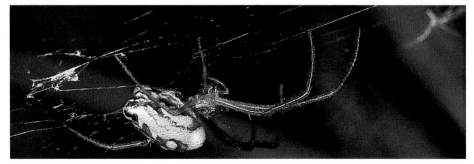

Silver marsh spider, Leucauge *sp.*

disturbed will move away quickly to nearby vegetation and hide by clinging, with legs outstretched, to a twig or grass stem.

Silver Marsh Spiders

Subfamily Leucauginae, *Leucauge* spp.

Web: Orb web with open hub, in vegetation. Webs can be more or less horizontal or vertically inclined. Capture threads are sticky.
Venom: Not known to be harmful to man.
Distribution: Throughout region, usually in damp places such as swamps and forests, but also in grasslands and gardens.
Description: Males and females are more or less the same size (7–16 mm). Long legs and silver, cylindrical abdomens truncated towards the rear and marked with reds, greens and gold. These spiders normally wait at the centre of their webs for prey. After the prey has been caught, it is wrapped in silk. They are sometimes the most numerous orb-web spiders in shaded woodland and forests, and their beautiful colours often catch one's attention.

FAMILY ULOBORIDAE

Feather-legged Spider

Uloborus plumipes

Web: Orb web, usually more or less horizontal. Capture threads are hackled, but this is not always easy to see. Stabilimenta may be spun in a variety of shapes.

Venom: None. The Uloboridae is the only spider family with no venom glands. Prey is rapidly wrapped in silk and covered with digestive enzymes.
Distribution: Widespread throughout the region. *Uloborus plumipes* is an introduced species, and is generally found in or close to human habitation, but other *Uloborus* species, which occur naturally in this region, are not restricted to man-made habitats.
Description: 10 mm or less. Carapace pear-shaped, abdomen has two humps. Very long front legs decorated with feathery bunches of hair. Colour pale brown or grey. Spider usually sits at hub of web with legs outstretched, resembling a piece of dry vegetation. Despite their lack of venom, feather-legged spiders can overpower insects much larger and more powerful than themselves. If disturbed, these spiders may drop out of their webs on a silken line.

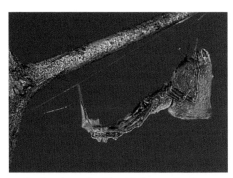

Feather-legged spider, Uloborus plumipes.

There are spiders in the families Araneidae, Tetragnathidae, Uloboridae, and others, that have abandoned the typical orb web altogether. Some of their webs differ so much from the original design that they cannot be recognized as orb webs (*see* page 42–43). There are even spiders in the orb-web families that do not spin webs at all. For example, at first glance the tropical tent-web spider's web does not seem to have much in common with the typical orb web, but after closer inspection one can recognize the central portion as a horizontal orb. Net-throwing spiders (family Deinopidae), which are related to feather-legged spiders, have also branched off the main stream in terms of web design: they spin small, rectangular webs, which are held with their front legs and thrown over their prey.

FAMILY ARANEIDAE

Tropical Tent-web Spider

Subfamily Cyrtophorinae
Cyrtophora citricola

Web: Complex (modified orb web) with fine-meshed, horizontal orb of non-sticky silk pulled upwards at the centre into a tent-like shape. Irregular scaffolding of threads above and below the orb, those above being denser than those below. A line of prey remains, dead leaves and egg sacs are usually suspended vertically from the centre of the web. Insects flying into the upper scaffolding are knocked down onto the catching web, where the spider grabs them.
Venom: Not known to be harmful to man.
Distribution: Common and widespread throughout the old world, tropics and subtropics, including southern Africa.
Description: Female: 8–20 mm, male much smaller. Colouring and markings vary from black with white and silvery markings, to various shades of grey, beige and brown.

Cyrtophora citricola

Web of Cyrtophora citricola

Paired tubercles found on the abdomen. Spiders can be solitary or communal-territorial in colonies of only a few to hundreds of individuals. Webs need strong supports, and are often built in large aloes and cacti. Dew-drop spiders, *Argyrodes* spp., live as klepto-parasites in the web of *C. citricola*.

African Bolas Spider

Subfamily Cyrtarachninae
Cladomelea akermani

Web: Reduced orb web: a trapeze or swing-shaped supporting web.
Venom: Not known to be harmful to man.
Distribution: Apparently restricted to the grasslands of KwaZulu-Natal Midlands and around Pietermaritzburg
Description: 8–10 mm; male much smaller than female. Colouring creamy yellow. Abdomen more or less spherical with raised, pimple-like tubercles. A line of stout, dark-tipped spines between the eyes, along centre of carapace. The front two pairs of legs are long and very hairy, resembling bottlebrushes. Nocturnal; during the day

this spider hides among its egg cases holding onto grass stems. Although the bolas spider is a member of the orb-web spider family (Araneidae), it has abandoned the conventional orb web. Instead, it has evolved an extraordinary method of catching prey. At dusk it constructs a trapeze between two points, hangs sideways from it, spins a single line

African bolas spider, Cladomelea akermani.

of silk with one or two large sticky drops at the end of it, and then swings it in a circular motion to catch moths. The spider almost certainly uses some kind of scent to attract its prey. Other spiders in this subfamily imitate the scent of female moths to attract male moths.

Hedgehog Spider

Subfamily Cyrtarachninae
Pycnacantha tribulus

Web: Reduced orb web: a trapeze or swing from which the spider hangs.
Venom: Not known to be harmful to man.

Distribution: Widespread throughout the region but rarely encountered.
Description: Female 10–15 mm, male much smaller. Golden brown with spine-like protuberances on abdomen, giving it the appearance of a spiky seed head. Front pair of legs long and strong, and armed with spines. Nocturnal, feeding on moths. Constructs a swing or trapeze of silk between two points, and hangs from it by the back legs, while the front legs are folded. When a moth flies past, the spider opens its front legs, and swings back and forth to grab the insect. It almost certainly uses some kind of scent to attract its prey. Other spiders in this subfamily imitate the scent of female moths to attract male moths.

Single-line Web Spiders

Family Uloboridae
Miagrammopes spp.

Web: Single line, middle portion of hackled (cribellate) silk.
Venom: None.
Distribution: Widespread throughout region.
Description: 3–10 mm. Rectangular carapace and long, strong, front legs. Nocturnal; hide in vegetation during the day, holding onto plants with their back legs and body while their front legs are outstretched, thus resembling thorns or twigs. Colouring cryptic, grey-brown or fawn. Use their bodies

A female hedgehog spider, Pycnacantha tribulus (*subfamily Cyrtarachninae).*

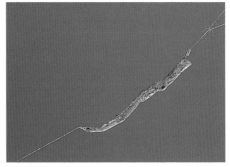

Miagrammopes *sp. uses its body as a bridge between two sections of its single-line snare.*

as a bridge between the two sections of their single-line snare; the line is held under constant tension and, by alternately flexing and jerking their bodies, the thread sags and then stretches to entangle prey.

Ogre-faced Net-casting Spiders

Family Deinopidae
Deinopis spp.

Web: A small rectangular web of exceptionally elastic, hackled (cribellate) silk is spun and then held between the front legs.
Venom: Not known to be harmful to man.
Distribution: Widespread in eastern parts of the region.
Description: Up to 20 mm. Cryptically coloured grey-brown and fawn. Abdomen cylindrical with paired tubercles; two front pairs of legs very long. Huge central eyes with acute binocular vision even in very dim light. Nocturnal, hiding during the day by lying on twigs, plant stems or branches with legs outstretched to blend with surroundings. At night they hang head down, suspended above the substrate from a scaffold of non-sticky silk, holding a rectangular catching web between their long front legs. They cast the web over passing insects with their front legs, then wrap them in silk with their back legs.

Ogre-faced net-casting spider, Deinopis *sp.*

Web of Deinopis *sp. (family Deinopidae).*

Humpbacked net-casting spider, Menneus camelus *(family Deinopidae).*

Camel-backed net-casting spider, Avellopsis capensis *(family Deinopidae).*

Identifying spiders

These one- or two-dimensional webs are flattish and generally more or less horizontal. The silk is usually not sticky, see page 42.

Sheet-web Spiders

Family Linyphiidae
Microlinyphia spp.

Web: Delicate sheet webs with no retreat; sometimes quite large for the size of the spider. Scattered threads form a scaffold above the sheet portion. Webs are built in vegetation, grass, shrubs, bushes and trees.
Venom: Not known to be harmful to man.
Distribution: Throughout the region.
Description: Small spiders, less than 6 mm. Males and females more or less the same size. Adult males have enormously enlarged pedipalps. General appearance dark and shiny, abdomen longer than it is wide and usually patterned along the side; front section of carapace raised, legs long and delicate. These small spiders hang inverted below the central sheet of their web. Prey is bitten through the web, and then pulled through it to be consumed.

Grass Funnel-web Spider

Family Agelenidae
Olorunia ocellata

Web: Sheet web of filmy, non-sticky silk leading to a funnel-shaped retreat in low grass or other vegetation, in crevices or in the entrance of mammal burrows.
Venom: Not known to be harmful to man.
Distribution: Widespread and common throughout the region.
Description: 8–12 mm. Abdomen tapered towards rear with long paired central spinnerets. Colouring dark brown to grey; the abdomen has paired lighter spots and leaf-like markings. This fast-moving spider lurks at the entrance of its retreat to monitor movement on the web. Because the web is not sticky, the spider has to react fast to intercept prey before it escapes. After the prey, which is often bigger than the spider, has been caught, it is dragged into the retreat. The female's droplet-shaped eggs sacs resemble small, sand-covered bottles and are hung in sheltered spots on a silken line.

Olorunia ocellata *in web.*

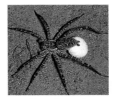 

Although similar in appearance, funnel-web wolf spiders, Hippasa *(Lycosidae)* (left), *carry their egg sacs attached to their spinnerets, while* O. ocellata *(right)* hang theirs on a silken line.

Velvet Spiders

Family Eresidae
Subfamily Eresinae
Gandanameno spp.

Web: Flat sheets of thick, dry, solid, greyish silk held taut with silken lines at the edges, covering an inner web of soft, fluffy, hackled (cribellate) silk. Web is often under the loose bark of trees or in crevices in masonry, rock exfoliations, etc. It extends beyond the spider's hiding place.
Venom: Not known to be harmful to man.
Distribution: Widespread throughout region.

Velvet spider, Gandanameno *sp.*

Description: 12–15 mm. Portly, dark-coloured (black, dark grey or dark reddish brown) spiders covered in dense, short hairs, appearing velvety. The cephalothorax is often darker than the abdomen and is blunt at the front; the carapace is slightly domed. The central pairs of eyes are close together giving these spiders a fierce, squinting look. Abdomen round-oval with parallel, paired dimples; legs short and stout. Female velvet spiders seldom emerge from under their webs, where they lurk, waiting for insects to touch the web. These are strong spiders that can overpower large insects.

Nursery-web Spiders

Family Pisauridae

The 'nursery web' in this common name does not refer to the spiders' catching webs but to the webs built around the egg sacs and newly emerged young. Not all nursery-web spiders build capture webs, many are free-ranging hunters. The members of subfamily Thalassiinae live near water, where they hunt small fish and other small aquatic animals.

Web-building Nursery-web Spiders

Euprosthenops spp. and *Euprosthenopsis* spp.

There are a number of genera of web-building nursery-web spiders.

Web: Large space web of non-sticky silk with wide, funnel-shaped retreat built in vegetation (often in large bushes or succulents), and also in the mouths of large mammal burrows.

Venom: Not known to be harmful to man.

Distribution: Widespread throughout the southern African region.

Description: 12–30 mm. Grey-brown spiders with long abdomens tapering towards the rear, marked with a darker leaf-shaped pattern on the dorsal side. Legs long, covered with spines. These fast-moving spiders hang inverted in their webs while waiting for prey. If disturbed, they will disappear in a flash into their retreats. Females carry their egg sacs under the cephalothorax, where they are held in her jaws and pedipalps. Just before the young are ready to emerge, the mother spider attaches the egg sacs to vegetation, spins a web around them and guards them until the spiderlings emerge. When they emerge, they bunch together under the protection of their mother until they are ready to disperse. At this stage the mother usually dies.

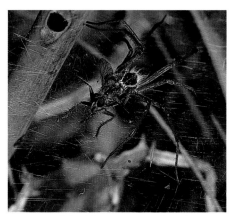

A web-building nursery-web spider,
Euprosthenopsis vuattouxi, *eating a robber fly.*

Identifying spiders

Female nursery-web spider, Rothus *sp., with egg sac. This spider is a free-ranging hunter.*

Community Nest Spiders

Family Eresidae
Stegodyphus spp.

Web: Irregular sheet webs of cribellate silk. These are spread out from a central 'nest' on various planes; large colonies can cover an entire tree in silk. The nest – consisting of strong, hard, cardboard-like silk and incorporating prey remains and bits of vegetation – starts off quite small but is enlarged as the colony grows, and has numerous holes and passageways. Birds that use spider silk in their nests, for example bulbuls and flycatchers, often break up the webs during the day, and therefore they have to be rebuilt every night. Webs are sometimes built on fences and telephone lines.

Webs of Stegodyphus dumicola *on a fence.*

Venom: Not known to be harmful to man.
Distribution: Throughout the region.
Description: 5–13 mm. Abdomen round-oval, cephalothorax blunt at the front with dark triangular markings on the 'face'. Colours soft, mottled browns and greys; males darker and smaller than females. Nocturnal. When a small insect becomes entangled in the web, one or two spiders will rush out, grab it, and drag it to the nest entrance, where more spiders will crowd around the prey to consume it. When a large insect lands in the web, even more spiders will converge upon it, until there is a heaving scrum of spiders which will eventually overpower most insects. There are also solitary *Stegodyphus* species which are bigger than the social species.

The male S. dumicola *(right)* is smaller and more brightly coloured than the female *(left).*

A solitary Stegodyphus *sp.*

These are complex, three-dimensional webs in a variety of configurations (*see* page 42).

Daddy Longlegs

Family Pholcidae
Smeringopus spp.

Web: Space web with a domed, central sheet and seemingly haphazard lines below and above. The central sheet may be decorated with white tufts of silk.
Venom: Not known to be harmful to man.
Distribution: Widespread throughout region.

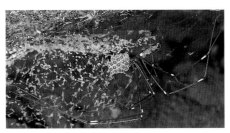

Female daddy longlegs, Smeringopus *sp. (Family Pholcidae), with eggs.*

Description: Body length up to 10 mm only, but leg span very large. Grey-brown with symmetrical darker patterns on dorsal side and yellow booklungs on ventral side of slender, cylindrical abdomen. Cephalothorax flat, almost circular. Legs very long and slender. Spiders hang inverted under domed centre of web and, if disturbed, flex their legs and bounce so fast that they become blurred. When taken out of their webs, they run with a strange bouncy movement. The female binds her eggs loosely with a few strands of silk, then carries them in her fangs. Newly hatched young cluster on her head. Some species thrive in undisturbed parts of human habitation, such as storerooms, outhouses, garages, etc. Others are found in the entrances of large animal burrows, the twilight zones of caves, under rock overhangs and in hollow trees.

Comb-footed Spiders

Family Theridiidae
Theridion spp.

This is one of the largest genera of spiders, therefore it is difficult to generalize.
Web: Space webs in a variety of designs, often with non-sticky 'runways' and sticky catching threads attached to the substrate. Many species construct a retreat in the centre of their webs, incorporating debris, prey remains, grains of sand, bits of vegetation or a curled leaf.
Venom: Not known to be harmful to man.
Distribution: Widespread and common throughout the region. Found in a wide variety of man-altered and natural habitats. Some cosmopolitan species commonly found indoors.
Description: 4–6 mm. Abdomen usually globular. Legs long and slender, third pair shorter than the rest. Spiders come in a variety colours: many are mottled browns and greys, some metallic. Some species have developed the most advanced methods of brood care among spiders – regurgitating partly digested food which the offspring suck from the mother's mouthparts. Others catch prey for their young.

Comb-footed spider, Theridion *sp.*

SPIDERS THAT DON'T BUILD WEBS

SPIDERS FOUND ON VEGETATION

These spiders are difficult to categorize and are found variously on grass, flowers, leaves, trees, tree trunks and under tree bark. They do not build webs, are free living, and although the majority are generally found on plants, some also come indoors, while others are found in a great variety of other habitats.

Rain spider, Palystes *sp.*

Rain Spiders

Family Sparassidae
Palystes spp.

Web: None.
Venom: Not known to be harmful to man.
Distribution: Widespread and common throughout the region.
Description: 15–40 mm. Large spiders with a leg span of up to 100 mm. Males and females about the same size although the females' abdomens are usually bigger. General colour fawn-brown with darker leaf-shaped pattern on dorsal side of abdomen, and black-and-yellow stripes on undersides of legs. Nocturnal, wandering hunters that live in vegetation but often come indoors to hunt insects attracted to lights; usually cause quite a stir because of their impressive size. Females lay 70–300 eggs in a greyish, cushion-like egg sac. The sac, covered with

Grass huntsman spider, Pseudomicrommata *sp., (family Sparassidae).*

Huntsman spider, Olios *sp., (family Sparassidae).*

leaves and held together with silk, is hung in vegetation and guarded by the mother. The spiderlings emerge after about three weeks and cluster together under their mother's protection before they finally disperse.

Long-spinnered Bark Spiders

Family Hersiliidae
Hersilia spp.

Web: None.
Venom: Not known to be harmful to man.
Distribution: Throughout the region.
Description: 5–10 mm. Body flat and abdomen heart-shaped; one pair of spinnerets much longer than the others. Legs long and slender, the third pair much shorter than the rest. The eyes are in a distinct pattern on a raised tubercle. Colouring varies considerably, even in the same species: from very pale mottled grey, through darker greys, golden brown, uniform brown to almost black, all the colours blending with the bark on which the spiders sit; some spiders also change colour within these ranges. Bark spiders are usually found on tree trunks where they sit flat against the tree, with their heads down, waiting for passing insects. They are very fast and catch their prey with a sudden rush. They then run around it, pinning it to the substrate with bands of silk extruded from the long spinnerets.

Female long-spinnered bark spider, Hersilia *sp.*

Tube-web Spiders

Family Segestriidae
Ariadna spp. and *Segestria* spp.

Web: None.
Venom: Not known to be harmful to man.
Distribution: Throughout the region.

Female tube-web spider, Ariadna *sp.*

Description: Long-bodied spiders (6–15 mm) found in various colours: from purplish or reddish black to yellowish or brown. The carapace is generally shiny, while the cylindrical abdomen has a covering of short hairs. The legs are held with three pairs facing forward and one backward. Tube-web spiders live in silken tubes spun in crevices in rocks, masonry, holes in trees, tree trunks, bark and in the ground. Females do not willingly leave their tubes, and can be seen waiting at the tube mouth for prey to touch the trip-lines. The trip-lines are not sticky and therefore do not hold the prey but simply alert the spider to its presence. Adult males wander. An unnamed species from the gravel plains of Namibia places pebbles attached to silk in a ray around its burrow; the reason for this behaviour is not known.

Ariadna sp. at the entrance to its tube, in a tree trunk. The trip-lines radiating from the mouth of the tube alert the spider to passing insects.

Identifying spiders

Jumping Spiders

Family Salticidae

This family includes many subfamilies, hundreds of genera and thousands of species. It is the biggest of all spider families and is found throughout the world.

Web: Very few species build webs.

Venom: Not known to be harmful to man.

Distribution: Widespread and common throughout the region.

Description: 3–17 mm. Colouring covers the whole spectrum, from plain to brightly coloured and patterned. The most conspicuous features of most jumping spiders are their enormous central front eyes and the manner in which they turn their heads to focus on anything that catches their attention. The carapace is blunt towards the front, and the abdomen is often smaller than the cephalothorax. The abdomen is usually short and pointed towards the rear but is sometimes also elongated or oblong. The legs are generally rather short but some species have very long front legs. Most jumping spiders are very hairy, and can be almost comically decorated with extravagant tufts and brushes, resembling anything from brush cuts, cheerleaders' pom-poms to bushy eyebrows and moustaches; some have iridescent hairs. Very few species build webs but they all spin sac-like retreats in which they moult, rest and lay their eggs. Most are free-living, diurnal hunters although there are some nocturnal species. Some jumping spiders mimic ants and wasps and one genus, *Portia*, specializes in preying upon other spiders. Some live

Jumping spider (Family Salticidae) feeding on a fly.

Note the long front legs of this jumping spider.

A male jumping spider with greatly enlarged pedipalps.

A striking zebra-striped jumping spider.

socially. Not all jumping spiders jump to get around: some run, some jump, and some do both. Because of their very acute vision, jumping spiders communicate by sight, using elaborate courtship rituals and threat displays consisting of various forms of posturing, and signalling with the pedipalps and front legs (*see* pages 24–25).

Crab Spiders
Family Thomisidae

A very large family found throughout the world, it consists of six subfamilies, many genera and hundreds of species.

Web: Do not build webs, except some New Zealand species.

Venom: Not known to be harmful to man but fast acting on insects.

Distribution: Widespread and common throughout the region.

Description: 3–23 mm. Most males are smaller than females. First two pairs of legs are longer and stronger than the last two and often have a series of strong spines. Apart from these features, overall body shapes and colours vary according to the lifestyles of the different species. Most crab spiders live on

African mask spider, Synema *sp. (family Thomisidae).*

Thomisus sp. well camouflaged on a tree trunk.

Runcinia *sp. (family Thomisidae).*

Yellow flower crab spiders, Thomisus *sp., mating.*

A flower crab spider, Thomisus *sp., eating a fly.*

Identifying spiders

plants but some also live on the ground. Grass crab spiders have long bodies, and their straw or mottled brown colours blend with their surroundings. Species that live on tree trunks are mottled brown and grey, and decorated with tubercles to resemble bits of bark. Spiny crab spiders are found in grass flower heads, and the small, round-bodied, short-legged seed crab spiders of the sub-family Bominae, live among seeds. Flower crab spiders are brightly coloured (yellow, pink, green and white), and several species in the genus *Thomisus* can change colour over the course of several days to blend with the flower on which they sit. In contrast with flower crab spiders, ground crab spiders are earth-coloured and drab. Perhaps one of the strangest crab spiders is *Phrynarachne* sp., a small spider with a lumpy, mottled white, grey and black body. It spins an irregular pad of white silk on a leaf, and sits at the centre of it, resembling a bird dropping.

Crab spiders sit and wait for their prey, and their venom acts fast on insects, enabling them to take prey larger than themselves. They do not crush their prey but use their fangs to pierce tiny holes into their victims' bodies through which they then suck the body fluids. Afterwards the outer skeleton is discarded in one piece. Crab spiders are very common and numerous on crops and garden plants, and play an important role in keeping insect numbers in check.

Lynx Spiders

Green lynx spider, Peucetia *sp.*

Family Oxyopidae
Green Lynx Spiders, *Peucetia* spp.

Web: None.
Venom: Not known to be harmful to man.
Distribution: Widespread and common throughout the region.
Description: 10–23 mm. Males similar in size to females. Overall green in colour with red or pink markings, and a darker leaf-shaped pattern on the dorsal side of the abdomen. Green lynx spiders can change their colour slowly to blend with the colour of the plant on which they live. The cephalothorax is long, domed and raised toward the front; the abdomen tapers to a point towards the rear. The legs are long and strong, covered with conspicuous spines, and taper towards the ends. *Peucetia* spp. are found on vegetation and are active hunters. Relying on their well-developed vision, they leap to catch insects as they fly past. A common sight during certain times of the year is that of females guarding their egg sacs by hanging beneath them,

Small huntsman spiders

Family Philodromidae
Long-bodied grass spiders, *Tibellus* spp.

Web: None.
Venom: Not known to be harmful to man.
Distribution: Throughout region.
Description: From about 7–15 mm. Long-bodied grass spiders, as their name suggests, are generally found on grass and have elongated bodies and long legs. The second pair of legs is usually longer than the other legs. Most spiders are straw-coloured with darker longitudinal stripes on the abdomen. Because of their shape and colouring they are not easy to see until they move. These spiders are free-living hunters.

Tibellus sp. guarding her egg sac built in grass.

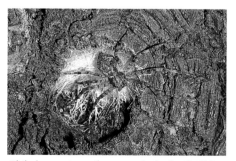

Philodromus is another genus in the family Philo-dromidae. This spider is guarding her egg sac.

Many spiders live on or in the ground, in burrows, under rocks and logs, in crevices in rocks, and under the bark of living or dead trees. Most of them are wandering hunters.

WOLF SPIDERS

Family Lycosidae

This is a very large family – worldwide there are more than 3 000 species and at least 29 genera are found in southern Africa. Most wolf spiders live on the ground, and are often found under rocks, stones and logs; some, however, also live on plants. They are ambushers and roving hunters, and some are semi-aquatic, running on water and diving under when alarmed. This group comprises both diurnal and nocturnal species. Funnel-

Wolf spider (family Lycosidae) showing its eyes.

Female wolf spider (family Lycosidae) with egg sac attached to spinnerets.

Identifying spiders

web wolf spiders, *Hippasa* spp., can be confused with the similar-looking grass funnel-web spiders, *Olorunia ocellata* – even their webs look similar – but wolf spiders carry their egg sacs attached to their spinnerets while grass funnel-web spiders hang their bottle-shaped eggs sacs near their webs.

Wandering, Burrowing and Trapdoor Wolf Spiders

Lycosa spp. and *Geolycosa* spp.

Web: None.
Venom: Not known to be harmful to man.
Distribution: Widespread and common throughout the region.
Description: 10–30 mm. The long cephalothorax is raised and narrower towards the front. Body is marked with longitudinal, alternating dark and light stripes. General body colour shades of brown and grey. Oval-shaped abdomen with light and dark symmetrical patterns on the dorsal side. Large chelicerae (fang bases) surrounded by red hairs. The central pair of eyes in the second row is very large, and its greenish-silver reflection is easy to pick up by torchlight. *Geolycosa* spp. and some *Lycosa* spp. hide in silk-lined burrows during the day. The burrow entrances often have a rampart of silk, reinforced with sticks or little bits of earth or debris; some spiders build trapdoors to close the entrance. Unlike true trapdoor spiders, they do not ambush their prey from the burrow but leave it to seek prey outside.

When they leave the burrow, the lid is sometimes discarded a few centimetres away from the entrance, and if they cannot locate it when they return, they will use any suitable object to plug the burrow. Like all wolf spiders, the females carry their spherical egg sacs attached to their spinnerets. After hatching, the young climb onto the mother's back, cling to her dorsal hairs, and only disperse after their second moult, when they are ready to start living on their own.

Buckspoor Spiders

Family Eresidae
Seothyra spp.

Web: *Seothyra* spp. do not build true webs, but construct vertical silk-lined burrows in sand, closed with a lobed cribellate mat built flat on the ground, which incorporates sand and is slightly concave in the centre. Two-lobed webs resemble hoof prints, hence the common name.
Venom: Not known to be harmful to man.
Distribution: Only found in sandy habitats in the drier parts of the region .
Description: Female 7–20 mm; male smaller

Seothyra *sp. burrow.*

Male buckspoor spider starting to dig a burrow.

Female buckspoor spider, Seothyra *sp.*

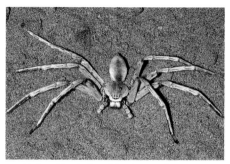

Male white lady spider, Leucorchestris *sp.*

at 4–8 mm. Female is fat and furry with short, stout legs, a raised carapace and an oval-shaped abdomen. *Seothyra* spp. are dark to light brown and grey in colour, and some have distinct abdominal stripes. Males are more brightly coloured than females, and some mimic large ants and wingless wasps in their colouring, shape and movements. Females hunt by waiting belly-up beneath the web for prey to touch the upper surface of the web. They are reluctant to leave their webs but adult males do wander in search of females. When the surface temperature becomes too hot or too cold the spiders retreat deeper into their burrows.

White Lady Spiders

Family Sparassidae
Dancing White Lady Spiders
Leucorchestris spp.

Web: None. Construct burrows which they line with silk and close with a silken lid. These are dug in flat 'dune street' areas or in slightly sloping sand to a depth of approximately 35 cm.
Venom: Not known to be harmful to man.
Distribution: Recorded as occurring only in Angola and Namibia but distribution is probably much wider in dune fields across the dry western parts of southern Africa.
Description: Up to 40 mm; leg span up to 100 mm. Large white spiders with long legs held at right angles to the body. Males and females about the same size. Nocturnal,

free-ranging hunters feeding mostly on insects but also on geckos, scorpions and other spiders.

Wheeling Spiders

Carparachne spp.

Web: None. Silk-lined burrows built in the shifting sands of dune slip-faces. Up to 50 cm deep, and closed with lids.
Venom: Not known to be harmful to man.
Distribution: Recorded as occurring only in the Namib Desert, Namibia.
Description: Up to 20 mm; males and females about the same size. Nocturnal, free-ranging hunters. Preyed upon by large pompilid wasps, *Carparachne* spp. have evolved a unique escape mechanism: when their enemy is in sight, they 'wheel' down sand dunes.

Golden wheeling spider, Carparachne aureoflava.

Identifying spiders

Burrowing Spiders

Family Zodariidae

There are four subfamilies within this family.
Web: None.
Venom: Not known to be harmful to man.
Distribution: Throughout the region in diverse habitats, but most numerous in dry regions.
Description: 2–21 mm. Most zodariids are dark-coloured, and many have a distinctive bluish-brown tinge. In most genera the carapace is narrower towards the front, and in those genera that dig, the carapace is high to accommodate digging muscles. The carapace can either be granular, shiny and hairless, or covered with rows of hairs. Abdomen shapes vary, but most are oval or elongate oval. The hind legs sometimes have strong spines. Most zodariids live on the ground, some 'swim' in loose sand, others dig burrows which they line with silk and close with a trapdoor, while others can be found beneath rocks or in leaf litter in forests.

The burrowing spider, Hermippus septem-guttatus *sp., lives in forest leaf litter.*

Flat-bellied Ground Spiders or Mouse Spiders

Family Gnaphosidae

This is a very large family with at least 25 genera in southern Africa alone.
Web: None.
Venom: Not known to be harmful to man.
Distribution: Widespread and common throughout the region.
Description: 3–17 mm. Sizes and shapes vary and colours range from pale fawn, grey and brown to dark brown, almost black. Many species have silky, shiny hairs on the abdomen. The most easily recognizable features are the pair of long, widely separated spinnerets, and the small, unevenly shaped posterior median eyes. All the eyes, except the anterior median ones, have a pale opalescent sheen. Gnaphosids are usually found on the ground and under stones, though some live in vegetation and roll up leaves to make retreats. Some species mimic ants.

Mouse spider, Camillina *sp.*
(family Gnaphosidae).

Orange Lungless Spiders

Family Caponiidae
Caponia spp. and *Diploglena* spp.

Web: None.
Venom: Not known to be harmful to man.
Distribution: Throughout the region.
Description: 6–13 mm. These spiders do not have booklungs, hence the common name. They breathe through two pairs of tracheae situated on the abdomen. The carapace is long and narrower towards the front; the abdomen is oval shaped. The carapace and legs are orange-yellow, while the abdomen is grey and covered with short, silky hair. One species, *Diploglena capensis*, has two eyes only, while the others have the normal complement of eight, set in a tight cluster on a dark area towards the front of the carapace. Lungless spiders are fast-moving, nocturnal hunters. During the day they hide in silken retreats under bark, rocks, fallen logs and in leaf litter or loose tree bark.

Female palp-footed spider, Iheringia *sp., in tube web with young.*

Palp-footed Spiders

Family Palpimanidae
Iheringia spp. and *Ikuma* spp.

Web: None.
Venom: Considered harmless to man but there has been a single anecdotal report of a bite causing medical problems.
Distribution: Throughout the region.
Description: 3–11 mm. Carapace granular and dark reddish brown with long silvery hairs; abdomen oval shaped, covered in short hairs, and often purplish or dark grey-brown. Legs same colour as carapace; first pair much larger than the others, each with an enormously enlarged femur. *Ikuma* spp. are slow-moving nocturnal hunters, preying on insects and other spiders. During the day they are found under rocks, etc., in retreats of sticky silk.

Male orange lungless spider, Caponia *sp.*

Scorpion spider, Platyoides *sp.*

Scorpion Spiders

Family Trochanteriidae
Platyoides spp.

Web: None.
Venom: Not known to be harmful to man.
Distribution: Throughout the region.
Description: 4–9 mm. Nocturnal, free-living and often found around houses. The legs are held sideways, with the last pair folding back over the abdomen. The body is flattened, enabling the spider to live in narrow cracks and crevices. Colouring varies from shiny red-brown or black to grey; the legs and abdomen are paler than the cephalothorax. The chelicerae (fang bases) are long, thick and widely diverging. *Platyoides* spp. are found in very narrow spaces under tree bark, exfoliations of rocks, flower pots and in narrow cracks in rocks, wood, masonry, etc.

Flatties

Family Selenopidae
Anyphops spp.

Web: None.
Venom: Not known to be harmful to man.
Distribution: Throughout the region.
Description: 6–23 mm. Free-living, fast-moving hunting spiders found on rocks, tree trunks and walls (inside and outside buildings), and often hiding in tiny cracks and crevices. Some species are mottled reddish brown on a creamy or light grey background, while others are much darker, almost black. Body is flat and legs held sideways in crab-like fashion. Females build flat, papery egg cases under rocks and bark, and against poles, roof beams and rough walls.

A flattie male, Anyphops *sp.*

A flattie female, Anyphops *sp.*

Fishing Spiders

Family Pisauridae
Subfamily Thalassiinae
Thalassius spp.

Web: None.
Venom: Not known to be harmful to man.
Distribution: Widespread throughout region.
Description: 15–30 mm. Big, robust, fast-moving spiders in various colours and patterns. Often dark brown or greenish brown with a distinct white band around the edge of the carapace. They move fast on water, dragging their hind legs as they run. Vibrations under and on the water alert them to the presence of prey (small fish, frogs, tadpoles, aquatic insects and freshwater crustaceans).

Female fishing spider, Thalassius *sp.*

Females hold their egg sacs in their jaws and pedipalps under the cephalothorax. Before the young are ready to emerge, the mother attaches the sac to vegetation, spins a web around it and guards it. When the spiderlings emerge, they bunch together under the mother's protection until they are ready to disperse; at this stage the mother dies.

Fishing spider, Thalassius *sp., catching a fish.*

Identifying spiders

The seashore spider, Amaurobioides africanus *(Anyphaenidae), with young. This spider is found in the same habitat as intertidal spiders.*

Long-jawed Intertidal Spiders

Family Desidae *Desis formidabilis*

Web: None.
Venom: Harmless to man.
Distribution: Along the coastline, on rocky shores between Lüderitz and East London.
Description: 18–22 mm. Head and chelicerae (fang bases) are dark red-brown, smooth and shiny. Chelicerae are enormous, about a third of total body length. Abdomen grey and covered with a thick pelt of water-repellent hair. The hair can trap an air bubble when the spider submerges, acting as an external 'lung'. The eyes are small but easily visible and in two straight rows. The legs are long and strong. During high tide intertidal spiders rest in waterproof silk retreats in empty limpet shells or in rock crevices. This is the only species of this family found along the southern African coast.

Long-jawed intertidal spider, Desis formidabilis.

APPENDIX

FINDING, COLLECTING AND PHOTOGRAPHING SPIDERS

If you really want to know more about spiders, you will have to start collecting them in order to identify them yourself or to have them identified by an expert. This means that you will have to learn how to kill and preserve spiders so that they can be examined microscopically. For identification purposes, spider specimens must be adult, and labelled with the following details: name of the spider (as detailed as possible, but family will do), exact locality (map coordinates are best), habitat (the more detail, the better), date collected, and the name of the collector.

There is a seemingly infinite number of spiders to be found, watched, photographed, studied and enjoyed. But, strangely enough, once you start looking for them, they seem difficult to find.

Where to find spiders

Spiders are numerous and common everywhere, but most of them are small, well camouflaged, nocturnal or hidden. It is therefore important to know where to look. Some spiders, like the brown button spiders, occur almost everywhere, but most spiders do have a preferred niche, and some species are typically found in specific habitats. Numerous other factors, such as weather patterns, seasons, latitude and altitude, also play an important role. It takes time and patience, but you will soon discover just how many different spiders there are to be found in our region.

There's no smoke without a fire, and also no silk without a spider – so when you start looking for spiders, look for silk and webs, but bear in mind that silk can outlast the spider that spun it.

Here follows a rough guide of all the places where you can find spiders, and also a list of which ones you can expect to encounter in these places:

In gardens: Button spiders, false button spiders, feather-legged spiders, flower crab spiders, garden orb-web spiders, golden orb-web spiders, jumping spiders, nursery-web spiders, orb-web spiders, sac spiders, silver marsh spiders, spitting spiders, striped garden spiders, wolf spiders, comb-footed and hammock-web spiders can be found in most gardens.

In and around your house, outbuildings: Button spiders, daddy longlegs spiders, dwarf round-headed spiders, false button spiders, false house button spiders, feather-legged spiders, flatties, jumping spiders, net-casting spiders, nursery-web spiders, rain spiders, sac spiders, scorpion spiders, comb-footed spiders and spitting spiders.

On and in the ground: Baboon spiders, burrowing spiders, burrowing wolf spiders, ground crab spiders, jumping spiders, small huntsman spiders, trapdoor spiders, trapdoor wolf spiders, wolf spiders and tropical wolf spiders.

In sand: Buckspoor spiders, burrowing spiders, jumping spiders, six-eyed sand spiders, wafer-lid trapdoor spiders, wheeling spiders and white lady spiders.

On rocks: Comb-footed spiders, flatties, huntsman spiders and jumping spiders.

Under rocks, logs, etc.: Baboon spiders, burrowing spiders, button spiders, comb-footed spiders, daddy longlegs spiders, dandy jumping spiders, false button spiders, false violin spiders, flat-bellied ground spiders, huntsman spiders, ground crab spiders, jumping spiders, mouse spiders, orange lungless spiders, palp-footed spiders, scorpion spiders, sheet-web mygalomorphs, spitting spiders, trapdoor spiders, velvet spiders, violin spiders and wolf spiders.

In grass: Bolas spiders, community nest spiders, crab spiders, garden orb-web spiders, grass huntsman spiders, grass spiders, grass funnel-web spiders, hedgehog spiders, jumping spiders, lynx spiders and silver marsh spiders.

On trees and shrubs: (On foliage, twigs and trunks, under the bark, and in holes.) Bark spiders, community nest spiders, crab spiders, dandy jumping spiders, kite spiders, golden orb-web spiders, huntsman spiders, jumping spiders, long-spinnered bark spiders, lynx spiders, net-casting spiders, ogre-faced spiders, orb-web spiders, pirate spiders, rain spiders, sheet-web mygalomorphs, single-line web spiders, tree trapdoor spiders, triangle-web spiders and tube-web spiders.

In wetlands: Fishing spiders, pirate wolf spiders, long-jawed water spiders, silver marsh spiders and orb-web spiders.

Along the sea-shore: Long-jawed inter-tidal and seashore spiders.

Equipment
While nothing beats the time-honoured method of turning over stones and logs, pulling bits of bark off trees and poking grass stems into holes to find spiders, there are some basic pieces of equipment that should make your task easier. The methods and

Astri Leroy with a white nylon sweep-net, ideal for collecting spiders. Shops don't sell equipment specifically designed for catching spiders; but most items are easy to acquire.

equipment you use are often a matter of personal taste, and depend on what kind of spider you want to catch, where you are looking for them and what you want to do with them once you have caught them.

Shops don't sell equipment specifically designed for catching spiders, but fortunately most of the items you'll need are quite simple to acquire and modify to your own specifications. The most basic and indispensable of these are small containers in a variety of sizes in which you can place your catch. Remember, if you want to keep the spiders alive, you can only put a single specimen in each container. You will also need a sweep-net for sampling grass, bushes and trees, a headlamp torch for spotting nocturnal spiders, and a small inexpensive jeweller's eyeglass. These are probably the most useful field tools.

Containers: It doesn't really matter what containers are made of, but small, transparent ones are best. Strictly speaking, transparent film canisters are too big for most spiders, but they are convenient, easy to acquire (film processors throw them away by the hundred), light, durable and if you want to keep the spiders alive you don't need to make air holes, as long as the containers are kept in a cool and shady place (such as a six-pack polystyrene cool box).

Sweep-nets: A sweep-net is ideal for collecting spiders from grass or the herb layer. The net must be strong because the aim is to hit the grass hard enough to dislodge spiders, and then to drag the net through the grass to collect them. A sturdy fish-landing net with a short, removable handle can be modified by replacing the netting with strong, lightweight, white material, such as nylon curtain lining. Nylon is useful because it does not rot when it gets wet. The seams must be flat to prevent spiders from hiding in them, and the material must be white, otherwise you won't see the spiders. It is a good idea to reinforce the edges with some stronger material to make the bag more durable.

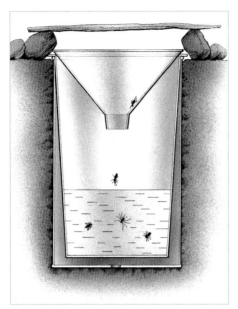

A pitfall trap containing preservative fluid will ensure that spiders caught will be preserved.

To dislodge spiders from bushes and trees, remove the handle, hold the net under a branch, and hit the branch hard with the handle.

Pitfall traps: These are useful for collecting ground spiders. To construct the simplest one, all you need is a can or jar and a smooth funnel that fits snugly inside it. Sink the can flush with the ground surface, remove the funnel's spout and place it in the can. Put a large flat stone or piece of wood, propped up with stones, over the trap and leave overnight. Spiders (and other creatures) seeking shelter will creep under the stone, skid down the funnel into the can, and will be unable to find their way out. This trap must be emptied once a day. You can lead small animals into the trap with 'fences' made of stiff plastic or a similar material. To ensure that rainwater drains out, punch holes in the base of the can. If you are unable to empty the trap once a day, place a jar in the can, and put glycol (a radiator coolant that does not evaporate) inside the jar as a

preservative. As soon as you remove the spiders, which will be dead by this stage, you can clean them off and put them in alcohol.

Tree traps: These simple traps consist of sheets of corrugated cardboard, which are wrapped around a tree trunk and held in place with a piece of string. A surprising number of spiders will creep under the cardboard, and can be collected without much trouble.

Spotlighting: Many spiders are nocturnal. Use a torch to look for them at night. In order to catch the reflections of spiders' eyes, the torch must be held at eyelevel. A headlamp is therefore the most useful. Hunting spiders' eyes, especially those of wolf spiders, can be picked up in this way.

Magnifying glass: Small, inexpensive, plastic jeweller's eyeglasses are ideal. A magnification of between 10 and 14 times is sufficient to see most field characteristics.

Other useful equipment:
- A small, cheap, water-colour paintbrush. You can use this to manipulate even tiny spiders without hurting them.
- A nasal spray or asthma spray bottle filled with water. Use this to spray a very fine water mist on webs, which will enable you to see every detail of the web clearly.
- A small spade and a sturdy screwdriver for digging out burrowing spiders.
- A small crowbar for moving rocks. Remember to put the rocks back where you found them.

Preserving spiders

Spiders' bodies are soft and decompose fast and therefore cannot be dried and pinned like insects. Instead, they are preserved in 70% alcohol. Labels, written in pencil or Indian ink, should be placed with the specimen in the bottle. Small spiders can be placed directly into the alcohol solution where they die quite fast, but larger specimens should be killed first. Ethyl acetate is ideal for killing large spiders fast without causing too much suffering. Select a glass jar with a wide mouth and a metal lid (ethyl acetate melts most plastics). Fill the bottom 2–3 centimetres of the jar with plaster of Paris. Once this has set, pour a few millilitres of ethyl acetate onto it, close the lid, and let it fizz. When the fizzing stops, the jar is ready. Drop the spider into the jar and close the lid; the spider will soon die. The fumes of ethyl acetate kill the spider, but being highly volatile, this substance evaporates fast and must be renewed every so often. When not in use, keep the bottle tightly closed.

Spiders in captivity

In South Africa it is illegal to import, sell or keep exotic (foreign) spiders, or any other arthropods, as pets. It is also illegal to catch, transport and keep any of our baboon spiders without a permit from the local provincial nature conservation department. If in doubt, check with the Department of Nature Conservation, a museum or the Spider Club (*see* page 93 for details).

One can keep spiders in containers but it is easier and more rewarding to observe wild spiders in their natural habitat. There is a great variety of wild spiders and, unlike captive ones, they feed themselves. Spiders that do not build webs or ones that build small webs can be kept in captivity, as long as their artificial home simulates their natural environment. They do not need large, elaborate cages – light plastic containers will suffice.

Remember to give the captive spider water. Most spiders only need a light spray

John Leroy preparing to photograph a spider, a waiting game which can take hours.

of water in their cage. Some spiders don't need water at all as they obtain sufficient moisture from their prey. Spiders don't need to be fed every day; once a week is usually enough. Finding the right kind of prey, and keeping it alive, can sometimes pose a problem. Spiders that build large orb webs cannot feed themselves in captivity because they cannot spin their webs in cramped surroundings. It is best to leave them where they are.

Photographing spiders

The equipment and principles used for spider photography apply to macro- or close-up photography in general. The most important prerequisite for photographing spiders, apart from the camera equipment, is patience. Spider photography is a waiting game and generally rewards those who can wait quietly for hours but are ready to roll when the action starts.

You will need a good Single-lens Reflex camera (SLR) with interchangeable lens capability, a built-in Through-the-Lens (TTL) exposure meter, and electronic flash synchronization. Nowadays, most SLR cameras have these features with a flash synchronization ability of $\frac{1}{60}$th of a second or faster. The most popular and the least cumbersome format readily available until recently has been the 35-mm-camera. However, with the advent of digital photography things are changing fast, and most cameras nowadays have full auto-focus capability. Unfortunately this is not necessarily always an advantage in close-up photography since the camera often focuses in the 'wrong' place instead of on the desired subject. It is therefore important to test your camera before you shoot a whole film on spiders.

A tripod with adjustments up, down and sideways is an absolute necessity. It must be light, strong, and not too bulky because you will often have to carry your camera equipment for long distances.

SPIDER FAMILIES OF SOUTHERN AFRICA

SCIENTIFIC NAME	COMMON NAME	AFRIKAANS NAME
Agelenidae	funnel-web spiders	tregterwebspinnekoppe
Amaurobiidae	hackled mesh-web spiders	deurmekaarmaaswebspinnekoppe
Ammoxenidae	termite-eating spiders or sanddivers	termietvretende spinnekoppe of sandduikers
Anapidae	ground orb-web spiders	grondwawielwebspinnekoppe
Anyphaenidae	seashore spiders	seekusspinnekoppe
Araneidae	orb-web spiders	wawielwebspinnekoppe
Archaeidae	long-necked spiders	langnekspinnekoppe
Atypidae	purse-web spiders	beurswebspinnekoppe
Barychelidae	trapdoor baboon spiders	valdeur-bobbejaanspinnekoppe
Caponiidae	orange lungless spiders	oranje longlose spinnekoppe
Clubionidae	sac spiders	sakspinnekoppe
Corinnidae	ant-like sac spiders	miernabootsende sakspinnekoppe
Ctenidae	tropical wolf or wandering spiders	tropiese wolf- of dwaalspinnekoppe
Ctenizidae	cork-lid trapdoor spiders	dikprop-valdeurspinnekoppe
Cyatholipidae	tree sheet-web spiders	boom-doekwebspinnekoppe
Cyrtaucheniidae	wafer-lid trapdoor spiders	dunpropvaldeurspinnekoppe
Deinopidae	net-casting and ogre-faced spiders	netgooi- of monsterkopspinnekoppe
Desidae	long-jawed intertidal spiders	grootkaak-tussengetyespinnekoppe
Dictynidae	mesh-web spiders	maaswebspinnekoppe
Dipluridae	sheet-web mygalomorphs	doekweb-mygalomorphs
Drymusidae	false violin spiders	valsvioolspinnekoppe
Dysderidae	long-fanged six-eyed spiders	langkaak-sesoogspinnekoppe
Eresidae	velvet spiders	fluweelspinnekoppe
Filistatidae	crevice weavers	rotsskeur-webspinnekoppe
Gallieniellidae	long-jawed ground spiders	langkaakgrondspinnekoppe
Gnaphosidae	flat-bellied ground or mouse spiders	platmaaggrond- of muisspinnekoppe
Hahniidae	comb-tailed spiders	kamstertspinnekoppe
Hersiliidae	long-spinnered bark spiders	langspintepel-basspinnekoppe
Idiopidae	spurred trapdoor spiders	gespoorde valdeurspinnekoppe
Linyphiidae	dwarf or hammock-web spiders	dwerg- of hangmatwebspinnekoppe
Liocranidae	spiny-legged sac spiders	stekelbeen-sakspinnekoppe
Lycosidae	wolf spiders	wolfspinnekoppe
Microstigmatidae	micromygalomorphs	mikromygalomorphs
Migidae	tree trapdoor and banded-legged trapdoor spiders	boom-valdeurspinnekoppe en streepbeen-valdeurspinnekoppe
Mimetidae	pirate spiders	roofspinnekoppe
Miturgidae	sac spiders	sakspinnekoppe
Mysmenidae	spurred orb-web spiders	gespoorde wawielwebspinnekoppe
Nemesiidae	tube trapdoor and wishbone trapdoor spiders	buisvaldeurspinnekoppe of vurkbeentjie-valdeurspinnekoppe
Nesticidae	cave cobweb spiders	grotspinnerak-spinnekoppe
Oecobiidae	dwarf round-headed spiders or star-legged spiders	dwergrondekopspinnekoppe of sterbeenspinnekoppe
Oonopidae	dwarf huntsman spiders	dwergjagterspinnekoppe
Orsolobidae	six-eyed ground spiders	sesoog-grondspinnekoppe
Oxyopidae	lynx spiders	tierspinnnekoppe
Palpimanidae	palp-footed spiders	tasterpootspinnekoppe
Philodromidae	small huntsman spiders	kleinjagterspinnekoppe
Pholcidae	daddy longlegs spiders	langbeenspinnekoppe
Pisauridae	nursery-web spiders	babakamerwebspinnekoppe
Prodidomidae	long-spinnered ground spiders	langspintepel-grondspinnekoppe
Salticidae	jumping spiders	springspinnekoppe

Spider families

SCIENTIFIC NAME	COMMON NAME	AFRIKAANS NAME
Scytodidae	spitting spiders	spoegspinnekoppe
Segestriidae	tube-web spiders	buiswebspinnekoppe
Selenopidae	flatties or wall spiders	plat- of muurspinnekoppe
Sicariidae	six-eyed sand spiders and violin spiders	sesoog-sand- en vioolspinnekoppe
Sparassidae	large huntsman or large wandering crab spiders	grootjagterspinnekoppe of grootdwaalkrapspinnekoppe
Symphytognathidae	dwarf orb weavers	dwerg-wawielwebspinnekoppe
Telemidae	long-legged cave spiders	langbeen-grotspinnekoppe
Tetragnathidae	golden orb-web spiders, long-jawed orb-weavers and silver marsh spiders	gouewawielwebspinnekoppe, langkaak-wawielwebspinnekoppe en silwervleispinnekoppe
Theraphosidae	baboon spiders	bobbejaanspinnekoppe
Theridiidae	cobweb and comb-footed spiders	spinnerak- en kampootspinnekoppe
Theridiosomatidae	ray spiders	straalspinnekoppe
Thomisidae	crab spiders	krapspinnekoppe
Trochanteriidae	scorpion spiders	skerpioenspinnekoppe
Uloboridae	tangle-web spiders	deurmekaarwebspinnekoppe
Zodariidae	burrowing spiders	grawende spinnekoppe.

GLOSSARY

Aerial dispersal: (also known as 'ballooning') a method of travel used by spiders – strands of silk, emitted from the spinnerets, are suspended by air currents, so carrying the spider through the air.

Antivenin: an antitoxin prepared from the blood serum of an animal (usually a horse), which neutralizes or inactivates a specific toxin.

Asexual reproduction: reproduction that does not involve sexual activity.

Bridge line: the first strong, silken line (usually horizontal) constructed by a spider when it builds its web. The rest of the web hangs from this line.

Calamistrum: bristles situated on the fourth pair of legs of cribellate spiders, used to comb out silk.

Capture threads: (or catching lines) the sticky or hackled threads of a web to which prey sticks.

Carapace: hard plate covering the cephalothorax.

Catching web: a web designed to capture prey, as opposed to, for example, nursery and sperm webs, which have different functions.

Cephalothorax: fused head and thorax as found in arachnids.

Chelicerae: (singular chelicera) fang bases.

Chemoreceptor: sensory receptor that responds to chemical signals, enabling spiders to smell and taste.

Compound eyes: eyes made up of numerous lenses (or ommatidia) as found in many insects.

Courtship ritual: stereotyped courtship behaviour between males and females of the same species which serves as a means of recognition.

Cribellate silk: (or hackled silk) silk produced from the cribellum of cribellate spiders and which is combed out with the calamistrum.

Cribellum: a plate, or paired sieve-like plates, from which fluffy, hackled silk is produced.

Cuticle: (or exoskeleton) hard outer layer of 'skin' as found in arthropods.

Cytotoxic: toxin that affects cells.

Diurnal: active by day.

Dorsal: of the back or upper surface.

Egg sac: mass of eggs, usually covered with silk in the case of spiders.

Endemic: restricted to a particular region.

Endite: segment of pedipalp nearest to the mouth.

Entelegyne: having complex copulatory organs.

Epigastric fold: crosswise slit on the underside of the abdomen.

Epigyne: hardened plate on the underside of female entelegyne spiders' abdomens in which the genital openings are located.

Exoskeleton: hardened outer skeleton or cuticle.

Extensor muscle: muscle that straightens a limb.

Flexor muscle: muscle that causes a limb to bend.

Fovea: a depression, pit or groove in the carapace where internal muscles are attached.

Hackled: *see* 'Cribellate silk'.

Haemolymph: spiders' 'blood'.

Haemotoxic: toxin that affects blood.

Haplogyne: having simple copulatory organs.

Insectivorous: insect eating.

Intertidal zone: the area on the seashore between the spring high- and low-tide marks.

Kleptoparasite: an organism that steals and eats either the host spider's food, young or web.

Labium: (plural labia) one of the lower 'lips' of the mouthparts.

Longitudinal: lengthways

Lyriform organs: groups of slit-sense organs in waved parallel patterns.

Metabolism: the process by which an organism converts ingested food to energy, which is used to sustain bodily processes.

Metamorphosis: marked physical change some animals undergo in the course of growth.

Nematodes: unsegmented worms, many of which live as parasites on, or inside, animals or plants.

Neurotoxic: toxin that affects the nervous system.

Nocturnal: active by night.

Nursery web: a web constructed around the egg sac by female spiders in the family Pisauridae.

Orb web: the 'classical' wagon-wheel-shaped web.

Oviduct: canal through which eggs pass from the ovary to the genital opening.

Pathogens: micro-organisms that cause disease.

Pedicel: the short, narrow 'stalk' that joins the cephalothorax and the abdomen of spiders.

Pedipalps: the second pair of appendages on the cephalothorax. In adult male spiders they are modified as copulatory organs.

Pheromone: A chemical substance or scent released by animals to signal information to others of the same species.

Radii: (in a web) straight lines of silk which radiate from the centre of a web to its circumference.

Retreat: a spider's place of hiding.

Sclerotized: particularly hardened (as referred to parts of the exoskeleton).

Scopula: (plural scopulae) tuft of hair on tarsus and sometimes also metatarsus of spiders.

Sedentary: moving about very little.

Seminal receptacle: part of some female spiders' reproductive organs where sperm is stored.

Sexual dimorphism: difference in body size, colouring and/or shape between the sexes.

Sheet web: a more or less horizontal sheet-like web, sometimes with a retreat.

Slit-sense organs: small pits, in the spider's exoskeleton, which are sensitive to vibrations.

Space web: a three-dimensional web which is not built against a substrate.

Sperm web: a small web into which male spiders deposit sperm from which to fill their palpal organs (sexual organs situated on the pedipalps).

Spinnerets: paired organs at the posterior end of the abdomen, through which silk is extruded.

Spiracle: a pore or opening in the exoskeleton where the tracheae open into the atmosphere.

Spirals: silk lines, usually sticky or hackled, joining the radii of an orb web in spiralling circles.

Stabilimenta: zigzags of loosely woven silk in various patterns; constructed in the webs of certain orb-web spiders, *see* page 62.

Sternum: hard plate under the cephalothorax.

Stridulation: sound production by vibration.

Substrate: any object or material on which an organism grows, rests or to which it is attached. In the case of spiders, generally the surface or object to which they attach their webs.

Tarsal organs: chemical (scent) receptors found on spiders' tarsi.

Tarsus: (plural tarsi) final leg segment furthest from the body.

Tergite: a hard plate covering a segment on arthropods' abdomens.

Tracheae: internal, cuticular tubes that make up part of the respiratory system of spiders.

Trip lines: threads that knock prey into the web or protect the web from damage.

Tubercle: small, dome-like projection.

Ventral: of the belly or undersurface.

Wandering spider: a spider that is not sedentary and not restricted to one place.

FURTHER READING

Carruthers, V. (Ed) 2002. *The Wildlife of Southern Africa.* Struik Publishers, Cape Town.

Dippenaar-Schoeman, A. & Jocqué, R. 1997. *African Spiders – An Identification Manual.* Plant Protection Research Institute Handbook no. 9, Agricultural Research Council, Pretoria.

Dippenaar-Schoeman, A.S. 2002. *Baboon and Trapdoor Spiders of Southern Africa – An Identification Manual.* Plant Protection Research Institute Handbook no. 13, Agricultural Research Council, Pretoria.

Dippenaar-Schoeman, A. & Van den Berg, A. 1988. *Common Names of Spiders (Araneae) of Southern Africa.* Koedoe, vol. 31.

Filmer, M.R. 1991. *Southern African Spiders – An Identification Guide.* Struik Publishers, Cape Town.

Foelix, R.F. 1996. *Biology of Spiders*, 2nd edition. Oxford University Press, United Kingdom.

Shear, W.A. (Ed) 1986. *Spiders, Webs, Behavior and Evolution.* Stanford University Press, California.

Smith, A.M. 1990. *Baboon Spiders: Tarantulas of Africa and the Middle East.* Fitzgerald Publishing, London.

For more information on spiders, write to the *Spider Club of southern Africa* at PO Box 2810, Wilropark 1731 or email **info@spiders.co.za**.

INDEX

Numbers in *bold* refer to visual material.

Index